ME

ME

BE DONE WITH
BROKEN RELATIONSHIPS &
A BROKEN LIFE

JUDITH DIALS

Dials Press
101 NW 197 ST
Miami, FL 33169

Printed in the United States of America

ISBN 978-0692878941

TABLE OF
CONTENTS

WHAT YOU'RE ABOUT
TO RECEIVE

ME was created to help women learn how to be done with broken relationships and a broken life. It was created so that women can get the relationship and life they've always desired. It doesn't matter if your past has left you broken. It doesn't matter if you feel scorned or if you're holding a grudge, pain, and anger inside of you. It doesn't even matter if your marriage seems to be headed for divorce. *ME* will help you with it all. All that matters is that you want more for yourself because you deserve more. So, if you want to end the broken relationships, the broken life, the hurting, the depression, and the stagnant place that life has brought you and begin to experience pure indescribable happiness and greater relationships, this book is for you.

Judith Dials is about to take you on a journey of a woman who started as a good girl and ended up in struggling relationships, unhappiness, constant rejection, depression, and loss of oneself. She thought she understood what it meant to love herself, yet her constant struggles proved her wrong. Nevertheless, she soon became interested in self-love after she realized that it brought her complete inner happiness; in addition, she developed a great relationship with her husband and a greater life overall. Throughout this book, you will learn ways to regain your happiness by replacing broken relationships and a broken life with pure inner happiness, better relationships, and a greater life.

ABOUT THE AUTHOR
JUDITH DIALS

Judith Dials is a wife, mother, author, relationship coach, speaker, and the Executive Director of Mature Enough (ME), an organization that teaches women how to be done with broken relationships, how to obtain greater relationships, and how to obtain pure inner happiness. ME was birthed from Judith's struggles with broken relationships. She always seemed to be the one left hurt, put on the back burner, or uncertain if the guy she was with truly loved her. She took a lot of emotional and mental abuse in those relationships. Even in the beginning of her marriage, she expected marital bliss, but instead received marital misery and loneliness because the relationship with her husband seemed like that of two roommates. She wasn't too happy during that time, nor was she sure if he was still interested in her. Consequently, they were headed for divorce.

While going through the rough patch in the beginning of their marriage, Judith dealt with things that a lot of women go through in relationships and life but are too ashamed to speak aloud. And, although she loved being a wife and mother, she was unhappy being *just* that. She felt something was missing. She was struggling with her identity, yet she was afraid to dream big or walk in purpose. However, all of that changed immensely when she understood that although she loved herself, she wasn't loving herself ENOUGH. That was the missing piece. Not only did this bring her pure inner happiness, but her life also changed greatly, and her relationship with her husband is now the best ever!

Extremely pleased with her success, Judith began teaching other ladies the steps she took to get where she is in her happiness. She has witnessed how their lives have changed through her guidance. In addition to forming Mature Enough, she also started a relationship coaching business and became a Relationship Speaker to women all over the world. Through these organizations, she teaches self-love to women in such a way that turns on a mental light bulb and allows women to see the areas where they need improvement. As a speaker, Judith's style is personable, relatable, and authentic. What she speaks is not just knowledge obtained through studies, but experience to understand her audience's mental, emotional, and physical state.

DEDICATION

This book is dedicated to everyone who has supported and inspired me. First and foremost, to my hubby, Chico Dials, whose wisdom is far beyond our time, because of your love, your patience, your wisdom, and the man of God that you are, God used you to help me be the woman that I am today. Thank you for loving me the way you do. I love you to the moon and back! To my handsome baby boy, Jeremiah King Dials who is forever my inspiration. My sister, Nancy Casimir, who first told me in my struggles to "just be happy." Unknowingly, that began my search for self-love. To my parents, Brisone and Rosiana Casimir, whose love I knew was never far. Finally, to my dear friend, Tamika Jeanty who has always been an inspiration to me since high school. From the day you told me you printed the words I texted you and placed it near your bed so you could read every day because it impacted you so much, I knew I had to share this message with the world. To all my family, friends, and supporters, each one of you has been an inspiration, and I love you all dearly.

This book, I dedicate to you...

PART I

UNDERSTANDING
ME

CHAPTER 1

ARE YOU READY TO BE HAPPY?

I used to be the kind of girl a man pursued, then as soon as I'd show mutual interest, he changed. Like, he'd start acting like a man who was never interested. However, because I liked him and wanted the relationship to go somewhere, I did everything I thought was right for him. But, it seemed like roles were reversed, and I was doing the chasing. Nevertheless, the relationship wasn't stable, and I was with him on and off. When he wanted to be with me, I'd get back with him. Likewise, when he didn't want to be with me, I'd be gone, and then the rollercoaster would start again. There were times when, I'd call and he wouldn't pick up…only when he felt ready. I'd wait all day for him to call. And yes, my mood was fixed on if I spoke with him or not. He definitely had control of my emotions. He basically seemed to be interested one day and the next he was not. Consequently, one day my mood was up. The next day it was down. I was happy, and then I was sad. I was in a rollercoaster of emotions.

I remember a woman telling me that I didn't love myself. I fought this notion for years! My very first thought was, *"What do you mean I don't love myself?!"* I went through the list of my accomplishments, where I was in my career, the fact that I owned my car, house, etc.… And, I couldn't understand why she said that I didn't love myself. Nevertheless, for years because I didn't accept that truth, my life kept crumbling. I remember telling that woman angrily, "I do love myself. I've got values; I see my worth!" I said that because I saw myself doing better than the people my age. I remember saying, "I don't smoke, I don't drink, I don't go to clubs, I'm still a virgin, and I go to church."

Of course, a lot of that changed as my life kept crumbling. Truth is, unfortunately, I didn't value myself enough because I allowed myself to be in a destructive, toxic relationship. I was dying on the inside. Yet, I stayed in a destructive relationship for years. I was prideful, and I was arrogant. I based my values off what society says is "good," which is why I thought I knew my worth better than other girls did…because I was a "good girl." You may be doing that, too. No one wants to face the ugly truth that they are causing themselves harm. No one wants to accept or believe that, because it'll only reveal that they are not loving themselves enough, which is an expression of self-hate that's almost too painful to accept.

I justified my self-hatred by putting the blame on the guy I was dating. I felt he shouldn't have awakened love until it was ready. It was easier to blame him. On the contrary, things happen to us because we allow it. It doesn't matter how much you say you don't like it or tell him to get out of your life; if you are physically still there, then you are allowing it. And... I, Judith, allowed it.

You don't want to be so prideful that you don't even take the time to examine yourself. Don't wait until years later like I did. Furthermore, don't wait until after you have allowed repeat destruction to your life before you realize that you weren't loving yourself enough. So many things can be avoided. Don't get me wrong, I have no regrets about my past because it brought me to where I am today. However, please understand that my life is not yours, nor is yours mine. The person I dealt with is not the same person you're dealing with. Don't ever look at how someone made it through their destructive relationship and think that it will work the same for you. No. Don't tempt or fool yourself. Don't stay in an unhealthy relationship just because you saw another woman do it and they eventually got it together. One woman can make it out okay and another woman just might not be as strong, can't take it, and commit harm to themselves. True story. I've seen it. I want to help you out of brokenness to become a happy woman with a happy life and a great relationship today.

Do you want to be happy? Sure, the question sounds absurd. You might be saying, "Who doesn't want to be happy?" I'm asking because although this may be what we want, unfortunately the journey to happiness sometimes requires a season of loneliness, some painful truths through self-examination, some splitting of friends, some time away from family, and some letting go of relationships. It may require you to be your only motivator and your only friend. Sometimes, the journey to happiness means a new location, a new mentality, and different interests. Thus, the journey may not seem all that happy in the beginning. It'll take you to a place where you'll have to be broken a bit more - even if it feels like you're already broken.

Sometimes we can be in the dark so long that we fear being in the light. It's as if we are unsure if being in the light is better. However, the best thing about being in the light is that you can SEE. You can see a *future*, see *better relationships*, see *financial prosperity*, see *happiness*, see *beyond where you are*, and anything else that you need to see. Believe me, once you step into the light, the journey will be worth it. As soon as you are in a place of happiness, you'll find that old friends want to reappear, and new friends will appear. You'll find yourself in a happy relationship. You'll find yourself pursuing things in life you never thought you'd be pursuing. You'll find inner peace.

So, I will ask the question again. Do you want to be happy? Or, are you too afraid of the process that you'd rather remain in brokenness, complaining and crying. Do you want to spend your days watching people who were where you are but are in a better place? Do you prefer to hold on to a relationship that is bringing you to your lowest in hopes that you can get him to change? Yet, we both know that no woman can change a man. Therefore, you may find yourself in that painful place forever. In fact, it can always get worse. So, are you ready to be happy? Or, do you feel that happiness is meant for someone else because the journey to happiness will have you leaving the things that you "believe" you love?

Remember, sometimes what you think is love is not love at all. It may be the pain of rejection disguising itself. That pain can be so strong that we believe it's love. We focus on the person that caused us that pain so much that we think because we can't get our mind off him, it must be love. Are you afraid to leave the pain? If love is causing you pain, then maybe you have truly become addicted to this painful love, and you enjoy basking in sorrow rather than joy. You urge for pain rather than peace. Maybe, just maybe, you have not realized that you have truly gotten comfortable with brokenness and allowed yourself to believe that you're happiest when you are in pain. Oddly, I have heard people say "there is joy in pain." Well, I beg to differ. I can see how you can have joy *after* the pain, but I can't remember the joy in pain.

I believe a part of you wants to be happy. Otherwise, you probably wouldn't have picked up this book. Still, is your heart ready to take the necessary steps your mind is attempting to make? Are you *really* ready to be happy? You see, the journey to pure, indescribable, inner happiness comes from understanding how to love yourself **enough**. If you choose to close this book because you believe you don't have any problems with self-love and that you have it all figured out, let me ask you one question. How has that been working for you? Most people believe they have self-love. They believe it's the least of their problems. However, the lack of self-love is proven through constant bad relationships, unhappy relationships, an unhappy life, not pursuing more or greater for yourself, not obtaining future goals or dreams, lack of peace, and so much more.

Then, there are good women who are constantly used by men, treated less than what they deserve, and connected in relationships with "bad men." These aren't always just the regular women who work regular jobs day in and day out. A lack of self-love can also be found in a doctor, lawyer, an author, a CEO of a great organization, or even someone with a thousand degrees who struggles with maintaining a relationship because they believe their accomplishments prove to be self-love. While these are great attributes, equating a successful career to self-love is one of the reasons why you hear a lot of women say that men are "intimidated" by a woman who is a boss and has degrees. This thought is not always true either. In fact, it is another sign of not loving oneself enough. (I'll explain that later in this book.)

The fruits of self-love are pure inner happiness, having great relationships with people and your spouse, financial prosperity, confidence, self-value, boldness, peace, and so much more. So again, I ask: Do you believe you have been loving yourself enough? If so, how has that been working for you? You can be like I was years ago when I allowed pride to make me think self-love wasn't my issue. Meanwhile, I watched my life continue to crumble before me. On the other hand, you can be honest with yourself and say, "Yeah, I want a better life than this. I want to know more." You may very well be a woman who understands self-love and the fruits are absolutely showing all over your life. I still encourage you to continue reading this book as everyone, including myself, needs continuous reminders, continuous growth, and continuous learning about self-love.

NOTES TO
REMEMBER

....

....

....

....

....

....

....

....

"Everything you want in life first begins with ME…
Yes, that means you."

CHAPTER 2

LOVING ME...
WHAT DOES THAT MEAN?

Loving me is self-love. Before I get into what self-love is, I want to tell you what it is not.

SELF-LOVE DOES NOT MEAN SELFISH.

I find that many women believe self-love means being selfish. They believe it means to forget about everybody else and the focus is all on self. No... that's a broken, scorned, or misinformed woman. On the contrary, I find that the more you understand how to love yourself, then you will know how to love others in the same manner. When you understand how to love yourself enough, you will know what it looks like to receive love properly.

Self-love isn't just about being a good woman or about being good to people. It isn't just about how well you groom yourself, maintain yourself, or upkeep your daily hygiene. It's not just about being a good wife, girlfriend, or person. It's not about how well you've done in school, the many degrees you've obtained, or the amount of money in your bank account. As a matter of fact, self-love isn't just about being the CEO of your company. You can have all the brains in the world and not love yourself enough. You can be the best wife to your husband and not love yourself enough. You can carry a thousand degrees, be a doctor, a preacher, or a president and not love yourself enough. It's not just about loving your flaws either. These are all misconceptions about what self-love truly is.

So, what is self-love?

Self-love means loving **yourself** to the best of your ability and knowledge. It is a **daily** reexamining and **daily** growth. The more you learn, the more you grow. It means doing good to yourself every day. Self-love means taking care of yourself spiritually, mentally, emotionally, physically, and financially. It means you are valuable, fearless, confident, content, a person of worth, and that you obtain power and greatness. You take **responsibility** of your life; what you are doing to it and what you are allowing to be done to it. It means a life of pure inner happiness and relationship. It means to respect oneself and others.

It is selfless. It means to give and do for oneself and in turn, have more than ENOUGH to give and do for others. Self-love means understanding WHO you are, WHY you were created, WHAT you are to do here on earth, WHEN and WHERE you are to do purpose here on this earth. It means to be in tune with everything the Creator has placed in you and has created you to be.

Self-love means to love who you are even if the world hates you. Love the perfect spiritual being that God created you to be even if the world claims you to be imperfect. It is understanding that you are a human being, living this life and learning as you grow. As you're learning, you will make mistakes, bad decisions, have flaws, and more. But, even with all that, you still speak highly of yourself, treat yourself well, and choose the best for yourself. You love yourself enough to know that your bad decision is not who you are, your mistake is not who you are, and your flaws are not who you are. All these things were but for a moment. Self-love is always choosing to be better than you were yesterday. Keep in mind that simply saying that you love your flaws and yet not trying to do better to yourself is a lack of self-love.

The Google dictionary describes self-love as "a regard for one's own well-being and happiness." In other words, it means that *(Insert Your Name)* matters. You matter. Your life matters. Your health matters. Your mental stability matters. Your finances matter, your goals matter, and your physical health matters. Everything about you, what you have going on, and your life's purpose all matters. And, if it matters, then it should be of importance. If it is of importance, then it should be treated as such and not always placed at the end of everything.

To obtain true self-love, you must make sacrifices. Both you and others around you may have to be uncomfortable temporarily so that the things that matter to you are attained. If you choose a life of comfortability with no regards for the need to change, you will find yourself helping others by giving all of yourself and all of your time to *their* needs, *their* importance, and *their* lack of responsibility. You do want to serve others, but please remember you are not a servant to man. You are a daughter of God, and you are worthy of a life of abundance.

Servants constantly do for others yet neglect themselves. I serve my husband, but I am not his servant. This means that I take care of him, and in the process, I am not neglecting myself. If you neglect yourself, you will find yourself completely depleted, drained, and eventually (if not already) unhappy. Why? Because you have not fulfilled what matters to you! It's not to say you're unhappy being a wife, mother, sister, friend, employee, etc. However, there is a balance to everything in life.

Be the best wife you can be! Be the best mother you can be! Be the best friend, employee, etc. But, do not neglect yourself and what is important to you in the process! When you're done being all of that to everybody and have neglected yourself, you won't have anything left for yourself. In fact, you can't be the best you in an unhappy, depleted state. If you're not the best "me" for yourself, then you can't possibly be the best "me" for anybody else. That is how I came up with the title of this book, ME. Because, "ME" matters. You must be intentional about making yourself better. Everything you desire in life first begins with, ME…yes, that means you.

Will you get to a point where you have completely reached a full understanding of self-love? No, because scriptures say that we are like Christ. Therefore, if you're like Christ and have the mind of Christ, there will always be more to learn and grow. Don't ever get comfortable with where you are. Always pursue greater. I believe everyone has love for themselves. I think it's almost natural. However, I do believe there are many ways that we are not loving ourselves *enough*. You'll find that I use the word *enough* a lot, because as mentioned before, self-love is growth. The more you know, the more you grow. It is not to be offensive and say you just don't love yourself. It is rather, an encouragement that you seek to love yourself to the best of your ability and knowledge.

NOTES TO
REMEMBER

....

....

....

....

....

....

....

....

"Everything you want in life first begins with ME…
yes, that means you."

CHAPTER 3

HOW DO I START LOVING MYSELF ENOUGH?

Everybody has their own ideas of how and where to find self-love. I must say that although I agree with some of the benefits, I can't always agree on where to find it. There should be a beginning. It doesn't just appear out of thin air. You can't just make it be a thing. I always say, when you want to find something in life, go back to the very beginning...which is the Creator who can literally make it plain and simple for you.

You can't truly understand how to love yourself unless you understand how much the One who created you loves you. I'm not talking about mom and dad. I'm speaking about the Creator...God. Too often we try to focus on loving Him and building a relationship with Him. However, that can be hard if we don't feel loved in return, if we feel like He's out to get us for every wrongdoing we've done, or if we don't understand the fullness or magnitude of His love for us. So, let's understand this first:

1. He loved us so much that He thought it to be right to create us in His OWN image. (Genesis 1:27) He didn't create us

like anything else of lesser value. No... He created us in His image. So, based off this alone, you already know that you are made by and with greatness. Furthermore, if He created us in His own image (knowing how great He is), what better demonstration of love is there? Well, let's continue because some people need more convincing.

2. He gave His ONLY Son to die for us so that we can have an opportunity to live with Him in Heaven. (John 3:16) This means that He forever wants us around. Now, that's love!

3. He felt it was His GOOD PLEASURE to adopt us as sons (daughters). (Ephesians 1:5) That is so that we don't come to him in fear as slaves but freely as a daughter because we ought to see Him as a loving Father. We have RELATION-SHIP with Him. Do you understand the benefits from a Father to daughter? Just think about how freely your child can come to you and ask you for something versus a child that isn't yours.

4. He has given us the power, the wisdom, the courage, the strength, and everything that His Son lived and walked in. As a matter of fact, He says, "As Christ is, so are we in THIS WORLD." (1 John 4:17) He also says that if we believe in His Son, everything Christ did on earth (which was pretty much GRAND), we can do AND greater. (John 14:12)

5. He said you are an HEIR. (Romans 8:17) You come from ROYALTY, which means you don't have to make believe anymore. All you have to do is truly believe.

He speaks so much more of His love for us in the Scriptures. Now, how easy is it to love someone who loves you this much? How easy is it to want to build a relationship with Him? Having a relationship with Him can give you better understanding of who you are, and you can learn how to bring out the greatness HE'S ALREADY placed in you. So now that you know you're all that and a bag of chips, how can you not have self-love?

If you KNOW you are greatness, then loving yourself should come naturally. It's a matter of BELIEVING it now. Truthfully, you are already valuable based off the information I've already given you. You can literally close this book and this may be all you need to understand self-love, your value, and your worth, which creates an inner happiness and a drive to release all brokenness. But then again, if you're like me - one who still struggled (probably because I didn't believe yet), let me encourage you to keep reading so you can know what also helped me.

Let's go back to the Creator when He was forming us. Please understand that every creation has a purpose - whether you know its purpose or not. If a musician grabs an instrument, he is creating music. For what purpose? It could be for entertainment, for money, or for whatever he chooses. An artist could draw a picture for a purpose. It could be for self-healing. I can go on and on, but remember, a creator creates for a purpose. I'm not sure what your beliefs are, but for me, the Creator is God. He created, the heavens, the earth, the light, the water, the animals, and every living thing. And as He was creating, He made sure to tell us that it…was…good! Then, He said in Genesis 1:26 NKJV, "Let us make man in our own image…"

Ok so God created man (both male and female). He immediately gave them purpose when He told them to take dominion over ALL the earth. Then, God told them to be fruitful and multiply, fill the earth, subdue it, and have dominion over every living thing that moves the earth. **He has given you purpose!** And, might I add, He looked at everything He made and said it was VERY GOOD.

Thus, the Creator, who is God, created you…with purpose, and you are already VALUABLE. Why? Because PURPOSE=VALUE. Value is defined in the Google dictionary as "usefulness of something." There is importance to it. There is worth to it. There is use for you. Your presence and what you do is important. Who you are and what you do has worth. Anything of value is held to a high estate. People cherish it, take care of it, want it, and like its presence because things or people of value, bring value to others. If it didn't, we wouldn't care for it. Hence, it would be of no value…invaluable.

Too often I see people struggle with not knowing their purpose; therefore, they remain in a stagnant place in life. Sometimes, people pick a talent out of many talents and call it purpose. Other times, we think our purpose is something that we're passionate about. The truth is that we don't always know. Here's the thing: God gave us all a "grand purpose" to take dominion over the earth. Begin to tap into that, and be in relationship with God so that you can discern what is not of God. There is value in purpose. Remember:

1. You are valuable because God created you.

2. You are valuable because of all that God has already placed in you as His child.

3. You are valuable because of the greatness that you are DOING, BUILDING, CREATING here on earth to ADD value to OTHER people.

Just knowing the reasons you are valuable isn't enough. You must **believe** it and **own** it. If you don't ACT, TALK, WALK, KNOW or BREATHE as someone of value, then you and everyone else will treat you as such...one who is of no value. You've got to believe it before they do. Too often we want others to see or confirm what we don't even see in ourselves. Why do we expect them to see us beyond what we see ourselves? We seek confirmation or approval from them as if they know us better than God the Creator. They can only judge you based off what they see now, which isn't always good. That's because if you don't believe that you are greatness, you're more than likely walking, acting, talking like someone who is less than. Only God can see beyond your today. I challenge you first and foremost to love God, believe all that God says about you, and believe in who He created you to be. This my dear, is the first step to self-love.

NOTES TO
REMEMBER

....

....

....

....

....

....

....

....

"Everything you want in life first begins with ME…
Yes, that means you."

CHAPTER 4

BENEFITS OF
LOVING ME ENOUGH

I don't know about you, but I was TIRED of being broken! I was broken in relationships, broken in finances, broken spirit, and broken in life! I was tired of crying, tired of feeling inadequate, and tired of feeling like I was not good enough. It wasn't until I understood how to love myself enough that I realized there were bountiful of benefits that I was just letting pass me by. Who knew self-love had its benefits?

Well, when I stepped outside of the spirit of brokenness, I had undeniable inner happiness because I was tasting the fruits of self-love. I was no longer the girl being kept up at night wondering if my man loves me. I used to question that before and during my early years of marriage. You might wonder why I was feeling that way after marriage, but trust me, a lot of us do. I was no longer the girl putting my all into a relationship and not getting back what I deserved. I was no longer the girl being disrespected or the unhappy wife. I no longer felt the constant need to check my man's phone. I was no longer the unhappy coworker.

The benefits of self-love come in many different wrappers. I had the courage to become my own boss, and I absolutely love what I do! I became a confident woman - a fearless woman. When I began to love myself enough, I realized that I had to start taking responsibility of my actions. When I did that, things began to open for me. I stopped with all the excuses. I stopped blaming past or current hurt on the other person. I stopped blaming my parents for the lessons they did or did not teach me. I stopped blaming the schools for what they didn't teach me. I stopped blaming my job for my unhappiness. I stopped blaming my spouse for my unhappiness in marriage. I stopped blaming my past for where I was. I stopped blaming and took full responsibility, because loving me means just that.

I understand for some women that may be hard to do. Taking responsibility may make you feel like you messed up your life or relationship. It may make you feel like you were stupid almost. Don't stay on the negative thoughts and mistakes of your past. The enemy wants you to stay there, but that's not your place to stay. Rather, taking full responsibility allows you to see the weaknesses you once had and prevent them going forward in future relationships and in life. Taking full responsibility allows growth.

I had to love myself enough to take full responsibility for the things that made me unhappy in my life. I knew that I had to be Mature Enough to do that. Thus, it allowed me to make the necessary movements or changes for my happiness. I no longer allowed people to control my emotions. Am I a robot who doesn't have emotions and nothing phases me? No. That's not what I'm saying. I am saying that when things occur in your life and you recognize it, that's when you take control of your emotions. If you don't like your job, yet you choose to stay, it's not your boss's fault, your spouse's fault, or your kids' fault. It's not your finances or the lack of time that makes you stay. Take responsibility. It's you. Now that you have established that, do what needs to be done so that you can have a happy career, goal, and purpose.

I used to blame the lack of time, the lack of finances, or my spouse for the need to stay in my job, and I was miserable. I had it better than most because I didn't hate my job; I just knew I had bigger purpose. But, I became uncomfortable being at my job. I had to understand that in life there is an opportunity cost. I had to give up something in exchange to obtain something else. In my case, it was my sleep. I stayed up late at night and wrote my book, newsletters, messages, and so much more.

I created a strategic plan that would allow me to leave my job in three months and still have an income. I began working on my purpose while everyone was asleep. It is not impossible! However, it wasn't easy. I had to put in the work. You may have to stop blaming the man you're with or your ex for your pain. Maybe he was truly interested in you in the very beginning of the relationship and something changed. If you're honest with yourself, you remember the change. He was different. His words and actions were different. Take responsibility for the fact that you chose to stay because you believed you could change him or that he would change on his own. Sure, he fed you words that allowed you to believe he still wants you, but you knew his actions weren't aligning. You chose to believe his words and not his actions because you wanted to believe. Take responsibility so that you can break the cycle. When you have no one to blame but yourself, you begin to do better. You make better decisions.

Take responsibility for where you are in life. Read a little more. Do some research. I truly believe that if you seek, you will find. If you knock, doors will be open. If you ask, you shall receive. Yes, this is very true! I had to seek, knock, and ask for ways to work on purpose and keep a living. In doing so, I found, the door was opened, and the Lord answered. In the beginning days, you will have to make sacrifices of time, sleep, TV, and outings. These sacrifices will only be for a short time, and they will make way for you in the future. It will all pay off!

I was married and unhappy! How many times have you heard that?! Yes, it's true. It happens to a lot of married people. You begin to feel as if your spouse is just your roommate. You love each other, but something is missing. There is constant arguing - most times about small things. You hold unnecessary grudges. You even feel insecure. I remember when we were at the brink of divorce! Constantly fighting. Never seemed to agree on anything. But, it all changed! It can all change! How did it change? I learned to love myself enough!

I had to take responsibility for the things that were occurring in my life. I had to stop trying to change my husband, control him, or blame him. I had to understand that I needed to do a work in me whether or not he decided to do a work in him. I had to stop! I'm not saying that I did everything wrong and he had nothing to do with our broken marriage. However, believe me, when I started loving myself enough, honey, I… became…happy.

Who knew fixing me could fix our relationship? All it takes is one person to make the first move. Now, was he making the effort? I don't really know. What I do know is that I was too happy to even notice if he wasn't trying. I was secure with myself, who I was, and where I was going. I was secure with all that God placed in me, as well as with my flaws and my strengths. I was even secure in knowing I am great no matter how my life looked.

A lot of times, our insecurities create issues that aren't even there but are made up in our minds. Once I found myself, I didn't walk in fear of him leaving me. Did I want him to leave? No, I loved him! However, once that fear left, my confidence grew. I didn't fear him leaving because I knew that if he chose to leave, based on my relationship with God, the past could never compare with the greatness that is before me. I rested with the fact that I knew my Father will always give me His very best. Yes, I was sad sometimes; I'm not immortal. Still, I didn't fear.

A woman of confidence is very attractive…she's fierce! So not only did I become happy, but my husband also became happy in the marriage. I literally woke up one day and realized this man *really* loves me! I love this man more than I've ever loved him before. As a matter of fact, he says I'm the best thing that ever happened to him. I feel my husband is the best husband alive! (I'm sure a lot of wives feel this way about their husband…as they should). I enjoy being in his space. This guy is so full of wisdom that sometimes when he starts speaking, I just pull out my notebook to take notes because what he speaks come straights from the Heavens.

Now, you may easily say, "Well, Judith, it sounds like you were the problem." Girl, believe me when I tell you I was not the only problem! I just stopped concerning myself about him doing his part. I stopped trying to make him change. I prayed for him, and then worked on myself! When you are happy with yourself, petty things don't even bother you anymore. So, that's most of your arguments out the door anyway. In addition, your happiness overflows to your husband.

Your inner happiness will begin to attract people. You'll find people wanting to always be in your presence. You'll find employers wanting to promote you. You'll find yourself going into interviews and people hiring you based off the energy they'll sense from you. Does this mean you won't have other emotions like feeling sad, mad, or your weird menstrual moods? No. You're human. What it means is that you'll have more control of your emotions. You'll find less things getting to you. You'll find that some things aren't worth your energy, so you'll let it go. You won't dwell on things much.

Since my happiness manifested itself, I notice that people enjoy being in my presence. I mean we can totally have different interests, different beliefs, and different lives, yet they enjoy being around me. There's just an unexplainable connection. Thus, your happiness is attractive. Confidence is attractive. A woman with goals is attractive. A woman of values, worth, and security is attractive. I guess I can say I became…attractive again.

Another benefit of self-love is that you no longer fear failure anymore. You see, the biggest thing about failure is not the failing part. What we truly fear is the thoughts others have about us if we failed. If no one saw us fail, then we wouldn't care about how bad our project or goal turns out. We'd just pick back up and keep going. Let's just use "falling down a racetrack" as an example. If you were running down a track and fell, but there were no witnesses to see the fall, you'd simply pick back up, check for any wounds, and keep running towards your target. However, if you fall in front of a crowd, you begin to feel embarrassed. You wonder what they're thinking, which makes you want to curl up in a ball. You may stop running. If you continue running, you may not run as confidently as you did before, because you fear the thoughts of others who assumed that you failed. Stop fearing failure.

Self-love places a confidence in you that allows you to see the future beyond what everyone can see in you. Therefore, because you know who you are, you know that the fall doesn't mean you failed. You'll just pick right back up with the same confidence that you had at the beginning of the race. You do so because you know who you are, you see your future, and you know there is no failure in it - no matter what it looks like in other people's eyes. Self-love not only helps us understand who we are in God, the greatness that is within us, or how unique we are, but it also prevents us from caring about or fearing the opinions of others. It allows us to be so confident and sure of who we are that nothing anybody says will affect us.

Self-love creates confidence. How much more confident can we be if we knew that we are fully capable and fully qualified to tackle the assignment in front of us! It could be a speech to a crowd, the ability to speak in front of a camera, or even the ability to build a plane. Can it happen at the blink of an eye? Yeah, sometimes it can. Other times, it takes research, education, sitting in a seminar, picking up a book, and creating time.

But still, you are not unqualified. Self-love teaches us to tap into the greatness that comes from God and dwells in us. Once we know WHO we are, WHOSE we are, and WHAT we are capable of, then confidence comes naturally.

Self-love builds self-esteem because you're all that! Why walk around like somebody that doesn't have anything going for themselves? You only do that when you don't know who you are and what you have going for yourself. It also builds self-value. You're not afraid of losing your job, your man, your career, your business, or whatever it is. It doesn't mean that you should start caring less. It simply means that you worry less. When you are walking in fear, your aura exudes just that. People can sense it, and it is only human nature to take advantage of someone that is afraid.

The same thing goes with relationships. Before I got married, I remember being afraid to lose a relationship. The guy I was with knew it, too. Oh, did he take advantage! Although the relationship was toxic and there were many times when I wanted to leave, he put fear in me that if I ever left he wouldn't come back. What a twisted reverse psychology to make me stay... but it worked. I feared him never coming back, so I chose to stay and accepted the toxicity.

Even in marriage, you can't fear losing your husband. Don't fear divorce. I'm not saying to be open to it; I said don't fear it. I'm just saying that even the one that loves you can naturally take advantage of you unknowingly. Again, it is human nature to take advantage of a person that fears, because we know we can use it to our advantage. Before you get upset about that, know that it is not just being done to you, but you do it to people, too. Just think about it. Most times we're unware that we're doing that.

When you have self-value, you will walk, talk, and act like a woman of value. Consequently, you will also be treated like a woman of value. You won't feel the need to be to be the aggressor because you think he's taking too long to make a move. As a matter of fact, if a man is pursuing you, you'll simply let him pursue. You won't feel the need to "break the ice" for him to quicken the process, because you understand your value. You won't feel the need to "take charge" in having him approve of you in his life. Instead, you will let him lead in pursuing you. You will let him lead in showing interest in you because a woman of value wants what wants her. You understand that if he does not want you, then you are of no value to him, and he will treat you as such.

I say all of that to say this...the benefits of loving oneself are endless. I'm finding out even today how much more benefits there are. Sure, you may want to skip the chapters that speaks of self-love and want to jump straight to the juicy part like "How to Attract the Man You've Always Desired" or "How to Keep a Man Interested," but I promise you, you will do yourself a big disservice. Those chapters won't be effective unless you truly understand how to love yourself enough. Girl, you're on your way to being done with broken relationships and a broken life. I'm happy for you!

NOTES TO
REMEMBER

....

....

....

....

....

....

....

....

*"Everything you want in life first begins with ME…
Yes, that means you."*

CHAPTER 5

WHAT'S KEEPING ME FROM LOVING MYSELF ENOUGH?

Ladies, somewhere in life we've been taught to want what doesn't want us, love a man that doesn't love us, chase after what wants to leave. Somewhere in life, we were taught how to give love to others, yet neglect ourselves in the process. We were taught that it was honorable if we stuck through our man's infidelity and inconsistencies - as if losing ourselves in the process deserves such honor. We give other women the words "you're a strong woman" after she chose to remain in a destructive relationship that nearly broke her. But, she was a weak woman for allowing herself to remain in a relationship that nearly took away everything even her sanity. At some point, we believed that constant fighting, pain, and rejection in a relationship is NORMAL. If this isn't what we believed, then the numbers would prove otherwise. These teachings have been obtained through society, media, music, schools, upbringings…basically through people. How or what you've been taught is in the past. From this day forward, IT IS TIME TO RENEW YOUR MIND!

Remember this: the writers, directors, producers, and entertainers have one main goal. Okay, they may have many, but this one is very important to them all: TO ENTERTAIN THEIR AUDIENCE. They all want to move their audience by creating different emotions and reactions to keep their audience coming back. No reaction = no emotion = no money. When you watch television, there is drama or conflict. And, wherever there is drama, there is no peace. Why don't they want a completely peaceful story? A peaceful story appears to be boring. People say that it is unrealistic; therefore, they don't connect with it.

The writers of the dramas want your emotions to go up and down. They want you to feel happy, sad, angry, and happy again. While watching these types of shows is okay sometimes, the problem occurs when this is what we watch daily. What should be taken as just a fictional show, we bring into our own homes in real lives. As a matter of fact, even reality TV has become so "boring" to some writers that they feel the need to create drama.

Like you, I used to hate when people told me that I should stop watching a certain show or stop listening to a certain song. In fact, I rebelled against it. I believed I was strong enough to control my own mind but was so unaware of what my subconscious mind was intaking. I'm not here to tell you what you can and cannot watch. What I am saying is that everything you watch or listen to is being placed in your subconscious. That's something you have no control over. If you are ever concerned about how it affects your life, simply be honest with yourself about your current state. How are your finances? How is your language? How is your relationship? What do you think about your relationship with Christ? Are you happy? Are you a thinker or do you flow with others' thoughts?

These questions and more can show you the effect media and music can have on your subconscious mind. I believe when we are placed in a pressured situation, our subconscious often takes over. Subconscious is defined as "a part of the mind of which one is not fully aware but which influences one's actions and feelings." Think about it. If you know right from wrong, then what is it that sways you to do wrong? It's likely your subconscious and whatever you fed it.

How often are we listening to music or watching a TV show that encourages bad behaviors, language, laziness, or unhealthy relationships? What about the people you hang out with? Truth be told…birds of a feather really do flock together! Don't fool yourself to think you're so strong that you can hang with them all day and not pick up bad habits. Your subconscious is doing it for you. Music is the best way for writers/artists to place pain. When you feel pain, you write. Some put it into music. "Pain to pain. Feel my pain. I need someone who understands."

We like to listen to sad songs when we're going through because we need someone who can relate, who can understand. The only problem with that is that it allows you to remain in your pain. It builds up the feelings that you already had and sometimes, it creates more anger, more sadness. Not every singer is taking you to healing. They may not be taking you to a better place. Rather, you may be sinking with them and not realizing it. "Pain to pain. Feel my pain. I need someone who understands." They want you to feel their pain. Be aware of the music you listen to and the things you watch because they ultimately remain in your subconscious.

Here is my point. You must be INTENTIONAL about loving yourself enough, because neither the world nor society will do it for you. Unfortunately, sometimes family and friends don't have the best intentions for you either. In addition, just because the media or radio gives you something, it doesn't mean you should take it. You don't have to listen to certain music. You don't have to watch the reality shows with ladies fighting constantly over a man who is fickle about them.

You're feeding your subconscious that it is not only normal to have a man who is unsure about you, but also that it is okay to fight another woman over that man. You don't have to listen to music that says, "You can't live without him, breathe without him, your whole world revolves around him." When you're constantly listening to that song and singing it while thinking of your man, you are feeding your subconscious to think of him as a god. God forbid this man leaves you. Then, you'll feel like you're pretty much dead, because you've set your subconscious to think that you can't live without him or breathe without him.

You have family and friends who are also a product of their environment. This means they can only teach you what they know, what they've been hearing, what they've been watching, and what they've been taught. What do they know? Does their advice mean they're right? I don't oppose sound advice, but please beware of who is giving it to you. If I am tuned in to a great leader who I receive advice or mentoring from (whether online or in person), I look beyond what I see and listen beyond what I hear. You see, although they come from a good heart, they may be teaching out of fear, out of bad experience, or out of pain. That may not always be good. Even if it is, just be aware of who and what you are tuned in to regularly.

You can also be a culprit that is keeping you from loving yourself enough. Sometimes, you hinder your growth, your happiness, and your ability to be done with brokenness. How? Well, a lot of times, we want people to accept us with our flaws and all. Sure, that sounds great and people carelessly throw that saying around. However, life is hard already. Relationships are hard already. Why attempt to make it harder by refusing to fix your flaws because you have embraced them to be a part of you. Did you forget that you are made perfect in the Lord? Did you forget that you ought to be better and seek better because you are better than your flaws? It's one thing to not know your flaws, but failing to turn it into a strength is simply laziness and a lack of self-love.

Do you not realize that your flaw can prevent you from getting that job, that client, that goal, or that man? Do you understand that your flaw can prevent you from reaching people? To get the things that you desire in life, you have to be mature enough to let go of the things that cause a hindrance to your growth. These may be your flaws. Be intentional about self-love! Love yourself enough to present yourself greatly because you will be most affected in the end. Do you have an attitude problem? Don't embrace it, fix it. Do you have commitment problems? Don't embrace it, fix it. Are you promiscuous? Don't embrace it, work on it. Are you very sexual? That's cool, but the world doesn't have to know…leave that for your man.

Embrace that you are sexual for your husband, but fix the part where everyone needs to know, because no respectable man wants to claim a woman that everybody knows is a freak. He truly only wants a freak in the bed. I'm not saying that you should use that as a tactic to get him though. Depending on the type of man that he is, he'll take what you're offering him (sexuality), use it to his advantage, and once he gets what he wants, he's done. He doesn't want anything else you have to offer. Do you wear your heart on your sleeve? I understand. But, don't embrace it, work on it. Typically, if you're emotional, then you probably need to spend some time loving on yourself and not jump into another relationship where they can possibly put fire to an open wound.

If you've been hurt in the past, work on it. Don't expect him to accept you with insecurities, pain, and drama. Work on it as a single woman before you get with him, because these flaws will increase when you get a man. They can even possibly push away a good man, and more than likely cause you to temporarily keep a bad one. Most times, people that are doing better for themselves typically attract better. And, if you aren't doing better for yourself, you'll attract what you are…someone that is struggling with self-love and embracing their flaws with no attempt to work on it. Consequently, they will not treat you well. Please take heed, because I know this to be true. If you have a flaw, don't embrace it…fix it! Be better! Do better! I promise you will see better!

NOTES TO
REMEMBER

....

....

....

....

....

....

....

....

"Everything you want in life first begins with ME...
Yes, that means you."

STOP HERE

Please do not proceed to Section 2 of this book because
I not only warn you, but I guarantee you that
anything written going forward will return void if
the first section is applied but not understood.

PART II

DONE WITH
BROKEN
RELATIONSHIPS

CHAPTER 6

HOW TO LOVE

All my life I have been taught the wrong way to love. When I got it, I mean when I *really got it*, my relationship changed immensely, and I changed how I viewed relationships. The bible says, "And you shall love the Lord your God with *all* your heart, with *all* your soul, with *all* your mind, and with *all* your strength. This is the 1ˢᵗ commandment. Because of this Scripture, I learned how to love, how to be loved, and it how to be free! The second like it is, "You shall love your neighbor *as* yourself. There is no other commandment greater than these." (Mark 12:30-31 NKJV) I believe so much that a marriage on the brinks of divorce can make it with this scripture. My husband and I were once headed for divorce. Now, we are two people who like each other. We're beyond just loving each other; we absolutely like each other, and we enjoy being in each other's presence. This is simply because we applied this scripture in our lives.

So, here's what hit me after reading it. First, I am supposed to love God with ALL my heart, mind, soul, and strength. Now ladies, can we keep it real for a second? When we get into a relationship and fall in love, don't we usually give a man our

ALL? When we get married, don't we typically give our husband our ALL? I'm talking about we entrust a man (husband or not) with ALL our heart, our mind, our soul, and our strength! We've just been taught to do that! This is a serious and delicate topic, so please understand that I don't take it lightly.

When you give your ALL to someone, even your husband, you create him to be your god. Let's say he goes on to be with the Lord, or God forbid a divorce occurs, you're left feeling as if there is no use for you anymore on this earth. You feel you have lost your everything because you have made *him* your everything; you have made him your life! However, Christ says He is your life! No human being should be given your all nor should you request they give their all to you. Let him reserve that space for God just as you should. Please believe that man (your husband included) will fail you, and their failing should not be your demise. I'm not just speaking about failing as in divorce. I'm speaking about what if they fail you financially? What if something occurred in life and they can't financially provide for the home? Then, you are completely broke and exhausted in every aspect exhaustion can occur. Does all your anger go to him because you entrusted him with your all to take care of the home financially? Yes…possibly. While you should get a man that can take care of you financially, you mustn't entrust your all and your future in his finances. By doing so, you will have made him a god of your finances.

What if he fails you by not loving you like he loves himself or how Christ loves the church? This is real in so many relationships. A lot of women believe that because they married a man, he is supposed to love her as he loves himself. Yes, he should; however, if he is struggling to love himself, he will fail to love you the way you deserve to be loved. What if he fails you by not making you happy, protecting you, leading you, or pouring wisdom into you? What if he chooses to leave you?

If you have given a man your all, you will struggle when it comes to hardships in the relationship. Without realizing it, you have made him your source, your ultimate provider, your peace, your joy, your life, and your everything. The hardest part of it all is that you've made him your god. And, if a god fails you, you feel as if there is no more left for you. You lose faith. Because you've lost faith in man whom you treated as a god, your faith in the real God becomes shaky. It'll be hard to trust in Him. Your mind is in confusion because, truthfully, you really entrusted in man. Instead of loving God first, and then others as you love yourself, you loved others first, then yourself, and then God.

When the scripture says that I should love others as I love myself, it means that I should love them with the same measure that I love myself. However, my problem was that I was loving others (husband included) *more* than I was loving myself. The good in me was giving, giving, and giving and hardly receiving what I deserved in return. I gave so much of my time, energy, mind, heart, money, and peace. Consequently, I felt drained, depleted, used, abused, useless, broken, and lost. The lack of love that I had for myself caused me to neglect myself in my giving. I left me behind.

Have you seen a woman who is struggling, grinding, and holding down the family as her man pursued his dream? She supports him in his every move. Then, it appears that as soon as he gets to where he wants to be, he leaves her and finds a woman who hasn't even touched the struggles she made to assist him in reaching his dreams? Don't you ever feel so sorry for that woman? I've heard this story one too many times. Here are my thoughts on this situation. That struggle…is real!

When a woman is trying to hold it down as he pursues his dreams, it's real! She's doing all that she can in her power to be the best wife for him. I've even heard some to sleep in their cars, live in hotels, and do what they must do because they both believe in his dream. Amid him pursuing his goals, however, things at home aren't easy for a wife. She's working hard at a job to hold down the home. She's coming home to take care of the kids, cook, and clean. In the midst, she becomes frustrated, exhausted, and drained! She gets into uncomfortable situations because of the stress she's under about what the family will eat the next day, where they may sleep the following month, and how they are going to get to and fro. She is stressed.

Naturally, stress can weigh on a person. It can cause you to be someone you don't even recognize. A woman like this will find herself continuously lashing out at her husband. She will begin to halfway support him and halfway want him to quit his dreams because she needs more help. It's not because she doesn't believe in him, but rather things have become too much for her. Nevertheless, because of different perspectives, a man can only see you as a woman who is now disrespectful and doesn't believe in his dreams. He sees you as an angry woman, which you may have become during this process. However, you know it's not you. Finally, he gets to where he wants to be in life, and he leaves the very woman that was there for him from the beginning. Why?! It's simply because this woman was loving him MORE than she was loving herself.

You may want to argue this point by saying, "Why would he leave? She was just being a help meet…a wife, a good woman!" Sure. In a woman's eyes, this is who she believes she was to him. Yet, in his eyes, the woman he sees today is a bickering woman, a disrespectful woman, an angry woman, a woman who's holding resentment, a woman who didn't believe in him, and a woman who has become bitter. This is also true because in the process and because of the stress, she has acquired these traits.

Half of you want him to repay you for all that you've done. Therefore, you carry a "you owe me spirit," and he senses it. At this point, the constant arguing has driven the two of you apart. He thinks you're angry, bitter, and disrespectful, and he no longer wants to deal with it anymore…especially if he doesn't need to anymore. It's a sad but truthful ending of marriage for a lot of women. Does it always end up this way? No. However, I've heard this scenario way too many times.

Why did I mention all of this? Here's why. This woman did not understand how to love her husband as she was loving herself. She didn't understand that if she's depleted and drained, it changes who she is. She becomes not only a person that he doesn't like, but a person that she doesn't even like or recognize either. As a wife, she misunderstood *helpmeet*. Yes, she is there to help her husband in all the ways that a wife can, but not to the point of losing herself. So, what is the limit? I can't tell you what your limit is, but if you are finding yourself that unhappy, depleted, drained, and stressed out so much so that you two are at constant war with each other and you can't breathe, then you have gone too far. At some point, you began to love him more than you were loving yourself.

When you are loving others more than you are loving your-

ME – JUDITH DIALS

self, you will be used and abused. Moreover, you will find your-self feeling lost in life. It is human nature for one to use some-one as much as they can. Does everybody do it intentionally? No. Pay close attention though. I'm not saying to be selfish, because there are times when certain things in our lives need more of our attention - a sick family, having to meet a dead-line, getting ready to launch a business, or whatever it is. Do it happily, willingly, and lovingly. What I am saying is that even in that process, do not neglect you! You matter!

So, how could this woman have been better to herself? How could she have loved herself better in this process? Well, she could've done something that made her happy like pursue her purpose, dreams, and goals. Typically, when you are working on something bigger than yourself, little things don't affect you as much. Also, if the weight was too much and she gave it up to God, yet the stress still became unbearable, then she should ask her husband to help more. If he refuses, then she should leave for her sanity, for her peace, and because she loves herself and her husband. Look, if it ever gets so bad that you both are being disrespectful to each other, you are in constant war, and mental and emotional abuse are occurring, leave! If all of that is occurring in the home, physical abuse is not too far behind.

One way or another, if you both continue to behave like that, someone is bound to leave. Will you wait until it's too late? When the damage is irreversible? Understand that it can always get worse. Now, I know some people want to jump ahead of me and say, "Is she advising people to leave their mar-riage?" No, I am not. Hear me well. When you have two peo-ple that are at each other's throats every day, there is no peace. Nothing you want to pursue in life can ever happen in a home where there is no peace. You can't prosper, you can't grow, you can't move forward because both of your minds are constantly consumed with anger or frustration at each other. You're always unhappy, and you guys won't have the mental stability to think straight or come together to pursue future goals.

So, does this mean you go straight to the divorce house? No! But, I do believe in two people separating for their sanity, for their peace, to get their spirit right, and to build their relationship with God to ask Him for directions on how to make peace in their marriage going forward. I believe two people like that need to be by themselves to find themselves again. Somewhere in their chaotic relationship, they lost themselves.

Does separation mean becoming romantically involved with other people? No! That's singlehood also known as divorce! Some would argue, "Well, separation opens doors to cheating." My response to that is if you are married but separated, and you are even considering cheating, then that was already in your mind. At some point, you've already entertained the thought while you were married. Being separated is an excuse people use to justify that thought.

When you were living with your wife and you guys were at war like that day and night, if cheating was already on your mind, being in that home would not have stopped you from doing it. No woman or man can stop anyone from cheating; it must be a decision made on their own. Besides, if you two are going at each other like that, more than likely you guys have already limited or deleted sex from your marriage. That's because although you may still love each other, you don't like each other. Therefore, not having sex in your marriage while you're separated cannot be an excuse to cheat either.

No man is worth you losing your sanity! I hear a lot of Christians say, "Well, separation is leaving the doors open for the enemy…for divorce." Well, if we can be honest with ourselves, if you are even considering divorce, isn't the enemy already there? If you guys can't live at peace with each other in the home, that proves that the enemy is already there. Why let pride (what an enemy can use) or fear (another thing the enemy can use) keep you from getting to peace, mental stability, and clarity from God (what the enemy wants to keep you from)? When you're in constant battle like that, trying to work together is almost always obsolete because one is always trying to fix the other. And, if one appears to not be putting in the work to reconciliation, the battle starts again.

Every time I hear people say that God healed their marriage, it's typically a working He did with them individually. I'm not opposed to marital counseling either. I just know that a lot of men won't go. Even in marital counseling sometimes, they're short counseling sessions, and you spend a lot of money. If you don't have enough money, you don't have enough time to get to the real issues, and all you've accomplished is telling the counselor what you hate about your spouse. That ultimately leaves you in a worse situation. Now, if it works, great! However, personally for me, I'd suggest people that are struggling in their marriage to seek individual counseling first. It doesn't matter if you have been the best wife to a man. It doesn't matter if you feel you did nothing wrong. It doesn't matter if he cheated and you didn't. Whether you were wrong or not, seek individual counseling, because I can guarantee that somewhere in the process, it left you feeling broken.

In your brokenness, you've developed ideas or personas that

allowed you to act out of character. You've probably gained some insecurities, and you've probably become someone you and others no longer recognize. Accordingly, failing to confront these issues will lead you to worse situations going forward. Your ability to make sound decisions will be affected. Likewise, one relationship can create a domino effect of wrongs in your life if you are not healed. Having said all of that, does this mean that you and your husband should separate as soon as you begin to have continuous disagreements? No. I think we should always leave the door open for God and seek His direction first. He may tell you that your situation isn't that bad, and He wants you to stay. I've seen where two people can reason together just fine. Just seek Him first.

Remember, before the two became one, they were two individuals. Therefore, individual healing is often necessary to resolve marital conflicts. Maybe two broken people came together and thought they could make a perfect one. But the last time I checked, broken pieces of glass can't be made one unless fixed. So, fix it. Fix you. And when you fix you, you have more than enough to give to others…to your husband. So,   we know not to love others more than we love ourselves. However, you don't want to love others less than you love yourself either. When you do so, you will use them and you will abuse them. Loving others less than you love yourself is selfish. It can't be all about you. You have to love others in the same measure that you love yourself…as you love yourself. Again, once you understand how to love yourself properly, you'll know how to love others properly.

SELF-LOVE IS INTENTIONAL!

Whew!

I spoke to my married folks. Now, can I speak with my single ladies? To those of you that want to be married, why haven't you made it your goal? Let me say it in better words. If you want marriage, why are you accepting less than marriage? Have you begun to love him more than you love yourself? To love yourself is to be all that the Creator formed you to be. If a desire for a husband is in your heart, perhaps in the book of your creation, marriage is in there for you. Believe me, if you ask God for a husband, He won't give you a man who is unwilling to commit. If you do end up with that type of man, that is your decision to keep him.   According to Matthew 7:9 KJV, "Or what man is there of you, whom if his son ask bread, will he give him a stone?" God isn't gonna give you a counterfeit. He will give you the desires of your heart. The only reason you keep a man who doesn't want to commit is because you chose to love him more than you love yourself.

Now, I'm not saying to be crazy with it. If he doesn't want to commit marriage to you after the first month, he isn't crazy, you are. Although I've heard some people make that happen, I wouldn't recommend it, but to each its own. A bad marriage can kill you...figuratively and literally. I find marriage too complex to make such a quick decision like that about your life. However, I also don't believe it takes forever. How much time you take is based on you. You will know. However, please don't let the desperation of marriage have you making quick decisions that could ultimately affect the rest of your life. Just because he's a "good man" isn't the reason to marry him. You may not be attracted to him. He may not be the "good man" for you.

I remember dating a "good man" for years, and I was never attracted to him. I wasn't attracted to him physically nor mentally. That took a big toll on the relationship, and I finally decided that I couldn't do it. Just because he's financially stable doesn't mean you should marry him. He can cheat on you, bring you diseases, or even treat you like a woman of no worth because he knows that's why you married him. That won't work either.

If you want a man of God, a protector, a provider, tall dark, and handsome (or however you like it), a man that "loves himself" should also be included on that list. If he loves himself properly, he can love you properly. If he loves himself, then he values himself. If he values himself, then he values his responsibilities as a man, which is to love God, love himself, love his as wife as Christ loves the church, lead his home, protect his home, provide for his home, and cultivate purpose that God has given to him. (Girl, get that kind of man, and you are set!) A husband is supposed to love his wife as he loves himself. If you are dating a man who appears to not love himself properly, don't expect him to love you properly. He will love you as he loves himself.

Although you want marriage, don't be quick to marry the wrong guy just to say you are married. On the contrary, don't be quick to marry the right guy just to say you are married. The right guy may not be ready to take on the responsibilities as a man to do all these things for himself, you, his children, and his home. Pressuring a man like that to marry you before he's ready may you leave you in a state of regret in the future.

You see, the very things you're going to desire IN marriage will be the same things he advised you that he needed to get together BEFORE he was married, but you were in a rush. Let a man be a man and prepare to be the best husband he can be. Does that mean that you wait around? Again, in my opinion, no. Sadly, a lot of women choose to love their man more than themselves. Therefore, they wait on these men forever. Then, they later find that sometimes that option leads to being friends with benefits, being the mistress (or the other girl), a baby before marriage, or a broken relationship because he may change his mind about the relationship or never truly intended on marrying you.

I'd suggest that you pursue purpose as your king comes along. He is on the way, and he will come along prepared. Love yourself, value yourself, and value a man in your life who understands his true responsibilities as a husband, father, and man. A woman of value understands that she needs to work on herself and to prepare herself as a woman, wife, and mother. Furthermore, she understands that a man who is mutually prepared as a man, husband, and father will come her way.

NOTES TO
REMEMBER

....

....

....

....

....

....

....

....

"Everything you want in life first begins with ME...
Yes, that means you."

CHAPTER 7

HOW TO ATTRACT THE MAN YOU'VE ALWAYS DESIRED

Let me get straight to the point here. I'm sure you've all heard the saying, "You attract what you are." I halfway believed this statement for years. It took me some time to believe that the saying is in fact TRUE! One day, after realizing how very true it was to my life, I accepted it and called it "The Mirror Effect." I called it this because it is as if you are standing in front of a mirror, and your guy is your reflection. Here is what I'm trying to say:

If you want to attract a certain kind of guy, then you must be a certain kind of woman. Sure, you want a man that has it together, loves God, is financially stable, values himself, values family, is a protector, leader, provider, etc. However, you should obtain these attributes as well. Of course, they may not match up exactly. For example, you may not be a physical protector, but you may be a woman who protects your home such as through prayer or taking care of the family. Basically, who you are, what you do, your values, your morals, your standards, your aura, and your energy should be in the same family as his.

I once heard someone say, "People are more concerned about HAVING than BEING." People want to have a man with money. They want a man who drives a certain car or can give them a certain lifestyle. They want a man who has a nice house. They want nice things. They want to have free vacations. They want to have things! Having nice things is not wrong at all. Desiring a man that is financially stable isn't wrong either. The problem is when we concern ourselves more about HAV-ING than BEING. It is then that we seek after a man that can specifically give us these things. This man can smell a woman like that from a mile away. He knows that her sole purpose is to "look" good rather than "be" good. Why a man would continue to pursue a woman that he believes is more concerned about "having" than "being" is another story for another day, but some still pursue.

The problem is now that he has her and obtained her by giving her the things she asked for, he begins to treat her a way she didn't expect. He begins to mistreat her. Why? Because of the mirror effect. He is simply treating her like she is already treating herself. He gave her what she wanted, but his decision to treat her as a woman of no worth was a simple reflection of the way she treated herself. She presented herself as a woman who concerned herself more about having than being. Value and worth doesn't come from what you have. It first comes from who you are, and he treated her accordingly.

A queen understands who she is; thus, she concerns herself with being more than having. She understands that things will come to her because of who she is. Sometimes, women aren't concerned about being the kind of woman that a man can love and respect. They would rather do what they feel they need to do to obtain the things they want…even if it jeopardizes their morality, their womanhood, their values, and their worth. See, you can try to portray yourself to be a certain woman, but you can't fake it. You can try to pretend, outwardly but you can never fake your inner person. Your aura, your subconscious, and your energy speaks way before you do.

How your man treats you is only a mirror of how you're treating yourself. Sometimes we like to look at a man for the pain they've caused us, but we refuse to look at the pain we've caused ourselves by first allowing them to treat us is such a way. We can't be mad at them for simply reflecting what we are doing to ourselves, nor can we control in what degree of pain they put us through. If we are still there, then we are first hurting ourselves by allowing it. Here are some common examples of when women allow a man to treat them less than they deserve:

1. Allowing verbal abuse:

- Have you been called out of your name?

- Has he used derogatory words?

- Is he saying hurtful words to break you?

2. Allowing emotional abuse:

- Does he take you through an emotional rollercoaster?

- Does he want you today and drop you tomorrow?

- Does he leave you feeling worthless?

- Is he always putting you down?

3. Allowing mental abuse:

- Is he controlling you?

- Is he keeping you from seeing your family?

- Is he trying to control your every move and your thoughts?

- Is he manipulative?

4. Allowing physical abuse?

- Is he physically attacking you?

Then, there are other ways women allow a man to treat them less than they deserve. An example of this is wanting to be in his presence so much that they are willing to be connected to him even though he's told them he doesn't want a relationship. Thus, she seeks or accepts friendship or being the other woman in hopes that he'll commit to her someday. She puts down her values, her morals, and her self-respect in exchange for love.

While dating, sometimes women know or even see their guy doing something out of line. Still, they won't say a word because they're too afraid that if they say anything, they'd get a negative response from him and make him grow further from them. Therefore, they accept the pain in exchange for his presence simply because they are loving him more than they are loving themselves. They want him more than they want happiness for themselves. Here's my point...I titled this chapter, "How to Attract the Man You've Always Desired," but I mostly spoke about why a man treats a woman so horribly.

Let me tie it together if you haven't already caught it. Again, it is the mirror effect. If you find yourself always dating the same kind of man - the cheater, the abuser, the disrespectful man and the list goes on, it is because that is what you are reflecting to him. Your aura, your subconscious, your energy could possibly be speaking that you are okay with this kind of man. It's probably in your subconscious that you can fix him. Your energy is probably exuding that you fear leaving him which is why he'll continue to do what he's doing because he knows you really aren't going anywhere. All in all, you're still there. Thus, the mirror effect shows that you'd rather keep him the way he is than to leave him for your peace, your self-respect, your values, and your sanity.

I remember a pastor saying, "If you keep attracting the same dogs, what are you barking?" Harsh, but true! Thus, when you are truly ready to attract a good, honest man of value, then you should first be this person. If you believe that you are already this woman but you are still attracting the wrong men, then I would go back and read Section 1, "Understanding ME." If you still feel as if you are not the problem, I can almost guarantee you that you are not being honest with yourself. If you believe you are being honest with yourself, it may be time to seek a personal therapist. There are certain things that we can't see in ourselves. Don't get angry or feel bad, a lot of us have been there. Like I said, I used to fight the idea that I wasn't loving myself enough because I was a good girl, did right by people and men, and I was honest. My pride wouldn't let me be better.

When I use the term "mirror effect," I'm not speaking about a physical reflection. I'm speaking about an internal reflection. It's how you speak about yourself. It's what you're doing to yourself, what you're allowing in your life and in your presence, where you go, and the words that come out of your mouth. It's your aura, your vibe, and your energy. We often get upset at the man we're in relationship with because he's not treating us like a queen. However, instead of pointing the finger to him, direct it to yourself first. Are you treating yourself like a queen? Truthfully! Most times, if we are overall unhappy with our mate, it is because they are doing something to us that we are first allowing to be done to us. It's just easier to blame them. It's never easy to say we're doing the harm to our own bodies.

So, back to the previous question. Are you treating yourself like a queen? Do you respect yourself? Are you allowing others to disrespect you? Are you taking care of yourself, building yourself, pursuing greater for yourself, and spending time with the Creator to build relationship for personal growth? Or, are you simply treating him like a king and forgetting about yourself...the queen? Remember, God made both the male and female, and the two need each other. But, if a queen neglects herself, then she will no longer *feel* like royalty. Most times we want them to see within us what we don't quite see in ourselves first. We want them to believe in us what we don't quite believe in ourselves first. News flash...they're only human. They are not the Creator. They can't always see you, know you, or believe in you before you see yourself, know yourself, or you believe in yourself.

In fact, don't leave it up to man to tell you who you are because man is never satisfied. He'll try to mold you and create you to be a kind of woman that he wants. Then, later he might not want that kind of woman anymore. Trust me, I know firsthand. I got into a relationship trying to find myself and allowed him to tell me and mold me to what he likes. I later found out that he doesn't even like that kind of woman. On top of that, a man truly loves a woman who knows who she is, and she is confident in who she is.

Please remember this. If you want to attract a good man, then be a good woman. If you want to attract a man of value, then be a woman of value. If you want to attract a man that respects you, then you will have to first respect yourself and not allow him to disrespect you. If you want to attract a man that wants a wife, then stop being with a man who doesn't want a wife right now. Stop *playing* wife to guys because you believe that will secure your position. Forget the foolishness of some modern time guys telling you that they "need" to know if you are marriage material. Don't feel obligated to constantly cook for him, clean for him, put your bills together, put something in your name for him, live with him, and sleep with him! None of that stuff will get him to the alter. Ask the many women who have done it and it returned void.

Why do you expect him to ask you to marry him if everything about what you're *doing* is saying, "I'm ok to do this without marriage"? It's not about what you say! It is what you are doing! You are telling him with your actions that marriage isn't that important to you. You say that you want a man that is good to you. However, are you being good to you? If he is cursing you out, putting his hands on you, bringing you down, taking you on an on-again-off-again rollercoaster relationship, please understand that he is ONLY being bad to you because you are first being bad to yourself. I'm reiterating this because it is important...YOU ARE ALLOWING IT!

Maybe you aren't allowing it with your words, but you are

with your actions. You are still there in his presence where he can do the hurting again. Too often women are not taking responsibility for their actions. They continuously blame a guy for "leading them on." Most times, he is telling you he doesn't want a relationship. He is telling you that you would make the perfect wife for some other man. Instead of taking that for what it is, a woman would rather stay close and attempt to change his mind.   Trust me, a man will ride on until he's told to get out. And, even when you tell him to get out, he'll attempt to come back...especially if it's easy. However, that doesn't change the fact that he has stated that he doesn't want a relationship. The minute a woman decides to take responsibility for her decisions (or lack of) in the relationship and the day she takes responsibility for not loving herself enough by allowing things to occur to her, she will get a breakthrough with being done with broken relationships.

If you want a man that has a relationship with Jesus, then you must have a relationship with Jesus. If you do have that relationship, then you'll be able to discern a man who has a relationship with Him from a man who tells you he does just to impress you. You want a financially stable man who will be able to take care of himself and his home. That's great, but are you a financially stable woman? You don't have to have all the riches, but are you able to take care of yourself so that you can be a helpmate to your husband? Should anything happen that would prevent your husband from working, will you be financially secure to help as a helpmate?

Don't worry about the small percentage of women that you see on media that appear to strike gold by being a gold digger, because it is exactly what it is...an appearance. They could be with the gold, yet are living an unhappy life in an unhappy relationship. Yes, gold can open doors for happiness. However, without inner happiness, gold can intensify pain. Therefore, you should ensure that you can support yourself and your family should the gold happen to run out.

THE MIRROR EFFECT IS REAL!

TV, media, and people have all taught us wrong. They taught us that to get the man we want, we must do countless things to please him. They told us that we should cook for him, set a candle lit dinner, run his bath water, dress a certain way, put on a certain perfume, have sex this way or that way, and be this kind of woman to him or that kind of woman to him. No, no, no! This kind of thinking will have your mind fixed on him all day and all night! You'll spend your whole time trying to be someone he approves of or likes. You'll create him to be a god because you'll constantly be seeking confirmation from him! He is not your Creator!

Now, don't get me wrong. You absolutely want to do things to please your man. So, go ahead and find out what he likes so you can please him accordingly. However, don't do it for approval or confirmation. Don't *consume* your mind of always pleasing him, because his appreciation is only temporary until the next act. You want a man to like you for you; not for what you can do for him. Thus, be content with who you are. Love yourself and be confident with who you are – no matter how that looks right now because self-love is always improving.

If you are in constant relationship with God and you love yourself, you'll be so vibrant that your man will have no choice but to love you for you. And, if he doesn't, then he'll leave.

But even then, don't be afraid of him or any man leaving you. Don't change what is important to your identity to keep a man around. Because, 1) you won't feel free in your own skin. You'll feel like you're walking on egg shells trying to please him so he doesn't leave. 2) He will never be satisfied or content with you because you're not satisfied or content with yourself. 3) Whatever is afraid leaves an open door to be used and abused.

Here are a few tips on how to attract the man you've always desired:

1. Truly understand the Mirror effect. Look at the guys you've been attracting and understand that there is something about you that is attracting these kinds of men. They may be guys who don't like commitment, cheaters, guys who are not financially stable, or guys who only see you as sexual. On the outside, you may be the total opposite of them. However, there is something on the inside, maybe from your past experiences that is attracting these kinds of men. We need to be healed if we want to attract the kind of man we've always desired. (Read Chapter 3: "How Do I Start Loving Myself Enough?" for more help.)

2. Love yourself enough to not simply accept everything that comes from a man. Don't lose yourself in exchange for love. (Chapter 4: "Benefits of Loving Myself Enough" and Read Chapter 6: "How to Love" for more help.)

3. Know who you are - the true you, the person God created – not what society has created you to be. (Read Chapter 3: "How Do I Start Loving Myself Enough").

NOTES TO
REMEMBER

....

....

....

....

....

....

....

....

"Everything you want in life first begins with ME...
Yes, that means you."

CHAPTER 8

HOW TO KEEP
A MAN INTERESTED

Often in a relationship (especially marriage), we find that our men are no longer excited about us. They appear to be standoffish, uninterested, bored, or that they pretty much have gotten used to us. We tend to get upset about it because we want him to feel that spark or that excitement that he once felt about us and showed us in the beginning of the relationship. We fear that this lack of interest that he is experiencing may get worse, and he may start seeking another woman. We hate the fact that his behavior has made us feel like his roommate.

So, what is a woman to do? How do we keep a man interested? Simple...BE INTERESTING!!! Interesting means to arouse curiosity, catch someone's attention, or hold someone's attention. If you have been doing the same old thing day by day, then of course he's lost interest, and you are in no way arousing his curiosity. You see they are so excited in the beginning of a relationship because they are still learning you; thus, the suspense has captured their attention.

Women tend to get a new hairstyle, new perfume, new outfit, or learn a new trick in the bedroom to keep their man interested. While that does work, that alone is not enough! What happens after you have physically aroused him? Now, are you mentally arousing him? Is your conversation interesting to him? I'm not saying it's not cool to talk about the latest things you've seen on TV, but another way to keep a man interested is to get busy with the things that you love and that keeps your interest.

Sure, I could say get into what keeps him interested, which is not bad for you to do so that you guys can have something in common. However, what keeps him interested may not keep you interested for long. And again, you can't pretend. Thus, get into things that keeps your interest such as your passion, purpose, gift, or hobby. Because if you think about it, when he first met you, isn't that what you were doing? Isn't that what got his attention? Weren't you working on your passion, purpose, gift, or hobby when he was first attracted to you? When he first met you, it was you doing you that intrigued him. He was trying to get to know you and what you had going on.

What is it that drives you and keeps you up at night other than your kids and your husband? What is the next thing in life that you want to pursue? Start doing that and watch how his interest comes back. Because now that there is something new going on with you, he's trying to learn you just like he did at the very beginning of the relationship. He wants to know what's going on in your mind and in your life. He's no longer able to predict your mind anymore. Therefore, you become a mystery as you were in the beginning of the relationship. Keep him in the loop, but always keep busy working on something, and he'll always want to know what is going on with you. As a matter of fact, you'll find that he'll want to cling to you a bit more.

When I say keep your man interested by staying busy, I'm not telling you to pretend to be busy. I'm saying staying busy not playing busy. It is a part of human nature for both male and female to get comfortable with something we see every day. It doesn't mean that they love you any less. Think of your favorite food. If you had it every day, you would probably get bored with it, and tired of eating it. But, start adding a little something different to that same meal, and watch how your interest for it will once again arise. When you're busy, it means you have something going on in your life. The mystery behind what you are doing can be very intriguing. He'll always want to converse with you to know what is going on in your daily life.

Here's the key…it is not a game. You shouldn't play busy for his attention or to keep him interested. If you are playing games, please understand that all games come to an end. You'll get tired of playing because it is not authentic and you're really not busy. Furthermore, you'll stop playing once you get what you want. The problem with that is, you'll have to start the game all over again. Moreover, you'll once again no longer be a mystery, and he'll get comfortable again. However, you can't be mad at his reaction because remember, you were just playing.

So, how do you stay busy? Well, you do so by walking in purpose, which is taking dominion of this world. God destined that for your life. So, go for it! Your passion, goal, ministry, whatever it is…go for it! It should be something that keeps you up at night, has your mind going, creating, planning, executing, changing lives, helping people, whatever that is…stay busy doing it! If you are single, I encourage you to pursue your goals to the fullest, girl! There are no limits and no boundaries!

If you're married, you can be a busy woman and still not be too busy for your man! Make sure you have your priorities in order. If you're too busy for him, then that's not marriage. Please understand there is a king and leader in your home, and you should respect him as such. Keep your home together and make it peaceful. Take care of your man. Take care of your children. Don't hold out on sex because you're too busy. You are a wife and a mother. Your family should come first. However, do not…and I repeat… do not neglect yourself! You may say, "Judith, I don't have the time." Yes, you do! You have to be intentional about the things you want in this life.

Women can naturally get caught up with work, come home, cook, clean, take care of the child, spend time with the husband, and then feel so exhausted by the end of the day that they fall asleep and haven't done anything for themselves that day. What you don't understand is that since we can easily get so caught up with everything else, it is important for us to plan our moment. We have to create time. We all have different schedules, different spouses, different children, and different lives pretty much. Accordingly, how I create time may not work for you. You must figure out when you will be able to create time to take care of purpose.

Here is how it is at my home. I'll use the example of when I was working in the corporate world since that is the story of many women. I worked a nine to five job. Then, I would come and be fully focused on my family. I cooked, played with our son, hung out with the hubby, put my son down at 10:00 p.m.

went to the gym, spent some alone time with the hubby, and from midnight to 3:00 a.m., I worked on my purpose. By 7:00 a.m., I was back up for my nine to five job. I had three to four hours a day to myself to build something grand. That amounted to twenty-one to twenty-eight hours a week!

Even if you can't stay fixed to that schedule, make one that works for you. If you miss a day or two (or even a week for whatever reason), don't quit. Get back to working on purpose. Not only will purpose keep your interest, it'll keep you interesting, and keep your husband interested. My husband was intrigued by my passion, hard work, and my achievements. He was attracted to the growth in me. He was proud of me. Subsequently, it brought us even closer. The mystery about what I was up to had him in constant conversation with me. He was interested in my life.

Most women tend to drop what they have going on as soon as they meet a man. You might have been in school, pursuing a business, creating an invention, opening a studio, making music, and doing a great job at it, too! However, when you meet a new guy, he becomes your focus. When you get married and have children, you tend to find yourself on a routine just to make life easier. Be mindful that a routine is predictable, and there is no excitement about what's coming next. A man can become uninterested when you give him all your time, your mind, and all of you. In addition, when you stop working on you, he stops working on you.

Remember, this is part of self-love. Since you matter, your goals, your plans, your career, and your purpose should matter. It is valuable because you are getting ready to change lives one way or another. Have a balance in your life. Take care of your family and take care of yourself. Keep yourself interesting by fulfilling purpose, passion, dreams or goals, and watch your man stay interested in you.

NOTES TO
REMEMBER

....

....

....

....

....

....

....

....

"Everything you want in life first begins with ME...
Yes, that means you."

CHAPTER 9

GOOD GIRLS FINISH LAST...NOT ANYMORE!!

The saying "good girls finish last" is typically true. Sure, you may want to argue with this statement. However, the saying is true for a lot girls. I believe "good girls" are the hardest to convince of the lack of self-love. I believe this because I was one of the good girls, and I hung out with good girls. We believe self-love equals good. We associate self-love with the good that we do for our partners and people. We associate self-love based off what society says is good or what the Bible says is good. And, if we are a Bible and law abiding citizens, we believe we have self-love. Truth is, you can be a believer of Christ and not love yourself enough. We look at our peers, and if we are doing better than they are, we believe we have self-love. We believe self-love means selfish.

Yes, being good is a part of self-love, but it means nothing if you misunderstand how to love and value yourself. A lot of good girls miss this because they've lived their lives always doing right by people, doing for people, taking care of people, and living up to people's standards and society's standards.

They feel the need to maintain those standards, so they get into the people-pleasing business. They do it so much so that when it comes time to doing something for themselves for their betterment, it might make others uncomfortable. And, because it may make others uncomfortable, they choose not to put themselves first in fear of losing people's approval of them, in fear of it appearing as selfish. Remember, they feel they have a standard to hold. Everyone told them they were a "good woman," which is why you'll find a lot of good women literally break their backs trying to please a man, doing right by him, and doing everything for him while neglecting themselves and ending up broken.

See, what you must understand is that if you've been a certain way to people for a long time, when you're ready to change for your betterment, they may become very uncomfortable because your change is now requiring them to change. Don't be upset when they are unhappy with your change. You have literally trained them to be a certain way with you. You have trained them to think that you'll always be available to them and that you will always do for them. You have allowed so many things that when you begin to change for your betterment, they won't be able to say or do certain things to you anymore. You have trained them. People will normally be initially upset with something that no longer goes their way because your change may require them to change.

This same thing happens with relationships. If you've been in an unhealthy relationship for some time, and you are at the place where you're loving yourself enough because you now understand that what you're receiving in the relationship is less than what you deserve, please understand that your partner will be uncomfortable. This means that what you've allowed him to get away with will no longer be something that you accept. Thus, he will attempt to make you feel guilty about this change.

Here are some of the characteristics of a good girl:

1. She's not into games, which is good. However, she's the type of girl that likes to break the ice. She initiates the first move. She thinks doing otherwise would be playing games. If she sees a man looking, she'll tell herself, "I'm going to break the ice for him. Make the move for him."

2. She's typically not rude or disrespectful. She cares for her man. She wants him to be into her. She wants him to be into her so much so that she begins to conform to what he wants her to be. Thus, she's not confident in who she is. She changes who she is in exchange for love. If he likes a girl this way, she'll be this way. If he likes a girl that way, she'll be that way. She is so interested in him that she wants him to be interested her. As a matter of fact, she wants him to approve of her. She wants him to WANT HER and to believe that she is his wife.

3. She's typically not materialistic; she's not into his things like money, cars, etc. She'll actually accept a man with no job or someone who's not financially stable. She's basically just into him...the man. She wants him to know that she's not in it for the money or what he owns. She wants to make sure he knows she's into him. She assures him that she has money and a car and can help him out until he gets himself together.

4. She doesn't ask him for anything because she is so self-conscious and afraid of him thinking of her as a gold digger. She likes to pay for things. She's always the giver.

5. She quickly turns into helpmate before the ring.

6. She drops everything she's doing when he calls. Whether her project, school, business, goal, etc., it all starts to die as she gets into the relationship.

7. She cares so much about his thoughts of her. She wants him to want her so much that she's very conscious about what she's doing, what she's saying, and if he is okay with it because she wants his approval.

All good women may not have all these traits; however, she may have two or more. This kind of woman can get the man, but unfortunately she doesn't always keep the man. If she does keep the man, she's typically unhappy because she's living a life that he wants… not a life where she is completely comfortable in her own skin. Here's the thing. This kind of girl loves herself and carries certain values. However, she's not loving herself enough nor is she valuing herself enough. See, a woman that is loving herself enough obtains value and confidence. She has such value and confidence in herself that she doesn't seek to be approved by anyone but God.

Here are the characteristics of a good woman who values herself. Notice how she handles things a bit differently from a "good girl" who doesn't value herself:

1. A woman of value is not into games nor is she the kind of woman that "breaks the ice." She wants a man that wants her because she understands if a man doesn't want her, then

she is of no value to him. Thus, she allows a man to lead in the initiation process; she lets him pursue. She's not stand-offish either. She can show interest with a smile or look his way, but she won't head over and approach him just because he was smiling. Again, she lets him lead because she understands if she has to lead from the start, she will always have to lead him.

2. She's typically not rude or disrespectful. She's into her man and wants him to want her, but not at the cost of losing herself. She is very comfortable in her skin because she understands WHO she is and the GREATNESS that lies within her. She knows that she is not one to be toiled with. She knows she is a woman of value and everything she is and does not only impacts her but her family and the many people she will influence. Thus, being approved by him is not something that concerns her.

The confident woman in her believes he will want her (I mean she knows she's all that and a bag of chips...lol). However, she understands that if she is not what he wants, then, that doesn't lessen who she is. It simply shows that he is seeking something or someone different. Just like you may choose pizza over a burger, there are different strokes for different folks. Some may think pizza is the best thing on earth. Some may think otherwise and prefer a burger (or a veggie burger), but that doesn't mean the pizza has lost its tasty flavor! As with a man, he may rather diamonds than gold, but it doesn't mean that the gold is invaluable. She does not conform to him because she knows she can only be who she was created to be...that's the best version there is.

3. She is not materialistic, but she does believe that she deserves nice things. She understands that if her God is great, then she is great. She's not a big spender where she loses control of her finances, but she does keep herself together. She values herself; thus, she only seeks a man who values himself as a man, a husband, and a father. She understands that a man who values himself, values his responsibilities as a man, a husband, and a father to be able to take care of himself and his home. She understands that if a man can't take care of himself, he won't be able to take care of his home. She's not a gold digger, but she awaits a man who has himself financially together. She understands that before God ever created woman, He created man and put him first in His presence in the garden of Eden. Second, he put the man to work by having him tend and keep the garden of Eden. Finally, God brought him a woman. Therefore, the woman of value believes in order.

4. She is not playing hard to get. Most times, she is literally just busy. She doesn't drop everything she's doing because she has a man. She understands how important her work is and places value on what she's doing because her plan is getting ready to change lives. She understands balance though; she's not all work. So, she respects her time and his by planning. If spontaneous things occur here and there, she can be flexible. However, they can't happen all the time or else she'll never get her project done, which is also a priority in her life.

The biggest thing about good girls is that they are typically people-abiding citizens, which means that anything that people consider to be good is what they want to appear to be. With wanting to be good in front of society's eyes, unfortunately you get to a place where you're not loving yourself enough by not allowing yourself to be who God created you to be - a beautiful, spiritually perfect yet imperfect human being. You're afraid to be yourself because you're afraid to displease others. You lose sight of what's important, such as your values. Not values based off how it pleases others, but values that are good for your spirit, mind, and soul, etc.

Sadly, therefore many women are unhappy in life and remain feeling broken. They choose to put themselves last for the good of everybody else. A good girl gets in the people-pleasing business, whereas a good woman of value is delivered from people. When you're constantly putting everybody before yourself, you'll always be the one left behind, which is why good girls finish last. Don't be that girl.

From this point on, girl, it's on you! I believe there are plenty of single men of value in various races living out here in this world. Don't create your world to be small because if you do, then it will be. I believe you should have the desire for a serious relationship first. If not, then your aura will loudly speak "just having fun." However, your aura can also loudly speak "desperation." To avoid that aura, get busy with doing something you absolutely LOVE! It won't remove the desire, but it will definitely remove the desperation because you will be focused on more than just a relationship. When women ask me, "Judith, what should I do when waiting on a man?" I say, "Stop waiting!" When you are waiting on something, you tend to keep your whole focus on the arrival. Thus, go out! Get involved! Do purpose but stay social! Go out and be social. Mr. Right is not going to come knocking on your door!

And, girl, get yourself together! Take care of your body, hair, face, nails, makeup, or whatever it is you do to get yourself on point...do it!!! One, because when you look good, you feel good, you give out good energy, and you're more social. You're not trying to avoid being seen because you don't want to be avoiding Mr. Right (think about it). Two, because truth be told, we do judge a book by its cover! So why do you fool yourself by saying he shouldn't worry about how you look, it should be the heart that matters. You do it! Honey, if you're out there not keeping up with yourself, you aren't giving him the opportunity to look at the heart because he can't get past the exterior. I'm just saying. Look good, smell good, and feel good!

I know some ladies that don't like to look in the mirror. Some that put themselves down because of their weight, their skin, what they believe is a deformity. Have you ever seen someone with something that appears to be a deformity to you, but because they absolutely love this thing about them, they've convinced you that there's nothing wrong with it? I've seen women who hated their weight, height, toes, big lips, stretch marks, moles, etc... But the minute they took what appeared as a deformity and loved it, most people don't even notice it anyway. And, if they do notice it, don't bother them because it doesn't bother you.

Listen, a woman that loves herself understands that when God created man, male and female, He created them in His own image. God's image is perfect! Don't let society tell you otherwise because God was there before they were even created. He matters. Period. Then, as soon as He created male and female, He gave you value and purpose. You should have so much confidence in who you are internally that the external has no choice but to follow!

If you know you're exceptional inside, then who you are internally will believe (no matter what society says) that you're exceptional on the outside. Just as much as you take care of your internal, you will take care of your external. That energy, aura, positive vibe, confidence, poise, and body language will exude on the outside and make you the baddest girl in the room. You better know who you are! Stop trying to fake the funk by getting dolled up on the outside and not knowing who you are on the inside. You can't fake the appearance of strength. Men can see right through you.

NOTES TO
REMEMBER

....

....

....

....

....

....

....

....

"Everything you want in life first begins with ME…
Yes, that means you."

PART III

DONE WITH
A BROKEN
LIFE

CHAPTER 10

BE DELIVERED FROM PEOPLE

Once I understood who I was and what God has placed me here on earth to do, I immediately had a better life! Did my current situation change? No…not right away, but my mind did! I was done with a broken life. I realized that I had to take responsibility of where I was today. I couldn't blame my upbringing anymore. I couldn't blame my past, my husband, nor my child. I couldn't blame anything or anyone anymore. I was simply using people as a crutch for my irresponsibility to be better in life. I didn't want to take accountability for my actions. I knew that my actions would reveal that I wanted less than what I deserved in life. My actions proved to be twisted, which would reveal that my mind was twisted and I didn't have it all together. And, I dare not let people think that I didn't have it together.

Still, why did I want less than I deserved? Truth is, I kind of did and I kind of didn't. I did want the best for myself, but proving to people that I already had it appealed more to me. So, I went the microwave route. I got a frozen meal fast, but it was missing the fresh homemade taste and the nutrients. So, I reluctantly ate it to fill my stomach. If we can be honest with ourselves, we tend to do that a lot. We tend to put what would be best for us aside because we want to go the quick and easy route, and we want to satisfy other's thoughts of us.

I once heard a wise woman named Tiphani Montgomery say, "Be delivered from people." That saying right there changed my life forever! You have to be delivered from people's thoughts, opinions, comments, and critiques! Although some of their advice may come from a good place, they might not all be good for you, which is why you should be careful who you allow in your mind. For example, you may get the wisest person in the world to give you their thoughts, opinions, and critiques on something you believe God has told you to do. Yet, what they tell you can completely go against what you believe is the direction God is sending you for your project. However, because you respect their thoughts, you choose to end your project or go the route they suggest. You can completely miss the message God gave you because you trusted in man and not Him. I'm not saying apply this to everyone that gives you their thoughts. However, I would caution if I strongly believe it is from God to me, I would go in prayer about that.

I believe the reason I wasn't taking a leap of faith about what I knew God called me to do was because of fear of failure. As I stated before, people aren't afraid of failure; they're afraid of people's thoughts of them if they fail. Thus, they remain safe to avoid people's thoughts. If we truly believe in our own ideas, then we should understand that with learning comes failures. You don't always get it right. That's life! It's just a matter of getting back up and doing it again.

Most times you get to your goal faster because you've learned from your mistakes. The problem is that we believe that people will call us stupid if we try again after failing. Therefore, we so desperately want to get it right the first time or don't attempt it at all. Thus, we remain in a job we don't like, suppress the gift that is within us, entertain our gifts to ourselves or our safe circle, and remain in a stagnant, unhappy, life. All because we are concerned about other people's thoughts - the same people who are not doing anything for themselves. The ones pursuing a goal aren't the ones doing the talking because 1) they understand the struggle, and 2) they're so busy with what they got going on that they don't have time to get into your business. IT IS TIME TO BE DELIVERED FROM PEOPLE!!!

Please understand that people will talk, but what they say comes and goes. Furthermore, it has no power over you unless you believe it. As soon as you said it was gone, it left and you kept it moving! The only way a person can break you down is if you don't truly know who you are. Take some time with just you and the Creator. He'll not only tell you who you are, but He'll also dismiss the thoughts you accepted from others.

Section 1 of this book teaches how I came to being delivered from people. It all started with self-love. As I mentioned, it's not that we don't love ourselves, it's just that we're not loving ourselves enough. I had to first understand why God created me, His purpose for me, and who He said I am. Secondly, because of understanding this, now it was easy for me to fall in love with Him and want a relationship where I am in constant communication with Him. Third, because of one and two, I absolutely loved myself and knew how to love myself enough.

It made me secure, and it brought out confidence. I saw my true value, and found purpose. I realized why my time is valuable. I realized why I am valuable. I realized why I should protect myself and why I should be free. Lastly, it taught me how to love others properly. In fact, because I loved myself enough by investing in myself mentally, emotionally, physically, and financially, I had more than enough to invest in others. If you don't get to a place where you are delivered from people, then you will find yourself being controlled by people. Remember, you can't serve both God and man.

NOTES TO
REMEMBER

....

....

....

....

....

....

....

....

....

"Everything you want in life first begins with ME...
Yes, that means you."

CHAPTER 11

NO ONE IS BETTER THAN YOU

As soon as I was in my journey of self-love, I knew that I had to pursue greater. Everything about my very being urged for greater. How could it not? All that I realized was already within me has been coming to life! Listen, you are born great, but if you don't accept that this is who you are, you will live as someone who is less than great and will receive less than great from people, from yourself, and from life. My God is great, so I consider myself a superstar! I'm not speaking in the vain way the world likes to use the word. I always say, "My Father is Super, which makes me super." He said in the Scriptures, "You are the light of the world. A city sitting on a hill can't be hidden, and when you light a lamp, you don't put it under a basket, but on a lampstand to give light to all." (Matthew 5:14-15) I just added the "star" because He told me to be the light. So, it was a done deal for me, I'm God's superstar. When you see or hear me, you'll know Him.

I realized that God literally equipped me with everything I needed for a better life. It was right in front of me, but because of laziness and feeling I wasn't good enough or smart enough, I allowed life to past me by and remained stagnant. I chose to judge myself by the greats and saw a destination of impossibility until it hit me that God is no respecter of persons. If He equipped one person, then I am equipped, too. (I didn't say I was *going to be* equipped; I said *AM* equipped). Once you change your mindset, you change your life. Most people believe they don't have what it takes, and they're waiting on God to equip them or give them a go. Personally, when He said, take dominion of this world, I heard the GO!

Some people wait for signs to make a move. Again, to me that is laziness, unbelief, or fear. Jesus pretty much said in the Scripture, "Unless you see signs and wonders, you won't believe." (John 4:48) As if His word isn't enough. A sign just may not happen for you. So, will it stop you? What if you create everything to be a sign? I remember when I began the organization, Mature Enough, I was on a strict budget to get things in order. My car broke down, and I told a family member it will literally cost me the same amount of money that I was going to use to purchase something for the organization. This family member advised me, "Well, maybe it was a sign that God doesn't want you to start it yet." Of course, because of where I was mentally, I disregarded her comment.

If I had believed that, all the women who are being blessed today by this organization would have missed it because I saw something as a sign to quit. Nevertheless, I made ways to continue to pursue the launch of the organization. Why? Because way before I started speaking to women, I *saw* myself speaking to women. My vision was as clear as day. I was in the shower one day, and I literally saw myself speaking to thousands of ladies. I wasn't asleep. My vision was clear, so my mission became clear.

As I continued my journey, I had to learn to not compare myself to others. I had to understand that everybody had their own individual journey, gift, style, and method. I had to learn not to think that someone was better than me. Again, God is no respecter of persons. If He equipped another, He has equipped me. I had to understand that perhaps this other person I was believing was better than me, was simply INTENTIONAL about seeing things happen in their life. Therefore, they dedicated time and sacrifices to pursuing great. All I had to do was be intentional about everything I wanted in my life because God has already equipped me.

No one can be better than you. How can they be? *You* are the only *you* there is! It doesn't matter if they're in the same field or teaching the same things. They are still not better than you are. I literally have seen chefs given the same number of ingredients to cook the same meal, and everyone had their own style. It all tasted different; the texture was even different with the same ingredient! Yet, they were all great.

They had three judges, and each chef had a judge that chose them! What I am trying to say is that who you are comparing yourself to may have a *version* of you, but they can't be a better you than you. The only time someone can be better than you, is when you are no longer being yourself, and you are trying to be like them. That's only because they are simply being the best at being themselves! The only reason you don't see yourself as great yet is because you haven't stopped being someone else. Spend time being yourself and seeing your greatness.

Open your minds. Don't set limits in your head. God is a GREAT GOD! He created this BIG WORLD - not just this area, this city, this state, or this country. He created this world! As much as someone may appear to be doing the same thing you are, you can only do it the way you were created to do it. Furthermore, you can only reach the people in this WORLD that you were created to reach! You are not for everybody, nor are they for everybody. So, don't think you have to compete because you've limited your mindset to a certain location or to certain people. Think bigger than that. Now, God is in the people business. If what you believe is benefitting only yourself, then you've missed it. Yes, you ought to love yourself and want the very best for yourself. However, if your purpose is not to help, build, influence, or raise up other people, then you will never go anywhere in life.

Remember self-love is not selfish. Self-love's biggest intent is to truly love yourself enough so that you can have more than enough to love others in the same measure. Again, God is no respecter of persons. He equips you so that you can equip others. He gives to you so that you can give to others. Yet, the minute you get into the selfish business, you have literally put a hold on your blessing card because there's nothing getting ready to be deposited there.

NOTES TO
REMEMBER

....

....

....

....

....

....

....

....

"Everything you want in life first begins with ME…
Yes, that means you."

CHAPTER 12

UPGRADE YOU

It's time to upgrade you! What do I mean by that? I've literally spent this whole book talking about the inner you. Now that we understand that concept, let's talk about the outer you. You are a good woman of value. Period. Never forget that. But, let me ask you... Would you spend good money on a new car if the paint looked bad? I mean, it's new. It's drivable. But. would you even test drive it? Aren't you already turned off by this car because of the messed up paint? In fact, you would probably try to negotiate its price, because you think the price should be lowered based on its appearance. You, my dear, have lowered this vehicle's value. Now, this car is still valuable. However, you - the buyer, the receiver - have lowered its value. THAT...IS... LIFE. Please, don't try to fight it. It is what it is. How much quicker do you think this car would sell if they fix the paint job? Most likely, it would sell for the original price it was valued for or better.

Here's what I'm trying to teach you, although I think you may have gotten the point. You are a woman of value. If you know this, then present yourself as such. Don't expect people to just know that you are. Don't expect people to see beyond how you present yourself. I know you want them to see the interior, but they can't get past the exterior. People are vain sometimes. When you present yourself right, you immediately have people's attention (without even saying a word). Now, they are simply waiting on you to open your mouth and speak.

Do you have to present a plan? An invention? Do you have to sell a product? Are you about to present to the board a new way to use medicine? Are you a public speaker and have something that will change their lives? No matter what it is that you have to say, because you've taken care of your exterior, you already have their attention. Let's hope with all that preparation you did on the outside, you've also prepared on the inside so that your words turn on a mental light bulb. Always...be...ready.

What does present yourself right mean? To some, it may mean for you to fix up your hair. For others, it would be make-up, clothing style, doing your nails and toes, or putting on perfume. If you're like me, it was all of the above because I like to be on point! Now, do you do this every day? Maybe not. Don't stress yourself out and make it law. You may not do this somedays, but don't let that be every day. There are other few things that I did to enhance my exterior. I had to go back to the gym because I realized that I am getting older and my metabolism has changed. I also had to watch what I was eating because you can't be your very best fighting diseases that come from food if you could help it.

Above all the other investments I made in myself, the most important was when I began to read. You must constantly be a student - a reader. I don't just allow life to teach me. I read to obtain knowledge as well. Ladies, in your many readings, please don't neglect the reading of the scriptures. Don't you always want to be in relationship with the One that created you in this magnitude? Don't you want to have a mind like His? Scriptures tell us that we have the mind of Christ. So, let's do just that...upgrade you. Don't let your inner work go in vain because you refused to believe that you have some outer work to do. Do the work; get the results.

NOTES TO
REMEMBER

....

....

....

....

....

....

....

....

"Everything you want in life first begins with ME…
Yes, that means you."

CHAPTER 13

HAPPY WIFE, HAPPY LIFE

This chapter might have been nice to put in the "Done with Broken Relationships" section. However, I chose to put it here because we are talking about being "Done with a Broken Life." If we can be honest, sometimes as wives, we are unhappy. Consequently, this makes us have an unhappy life. Let's see if I have it right... Most of us wake up early, fix ourselves up, fix up the kids for school, drop them off to school, go to a job that we may not be too excited about, pick up the kids from school, may have to stop by the grocery to pick up groceries for dinner, cook the dinner, play with kids, help them with homework, bathe them, get everything ready for the next day, entertain ourselves with our husbands, sleep, and start it all over again. You can add or remove some things, but for the most part, it's that kind of routine.

Meanwhile, there settles an unhappy wife. There can be many reasons for this, but in my findings, money seems to be it. Lack of money places a bit of stress on a woman because women like stability. But, it's not only about stability. Money also creates a bit of freedom that takes a work load off her. She may not have to worry about doing her own hair, nails, massages, or facials. Money allows her to get it done professionally. If she's too tired (because women do so much), and she doesn't want to cook for the night, it allows her to purchase dinner or hire a cook. She may even afford to have someone help her clean her home with all the kids she's got messing it up. It can assist her with maintaining her beauty or the ability to take some days off and vacation. Basically, money allows a bit of freedom.

Another reason I'm finding that wives are unhappy is because in all her doing, she has not taken time for herself to do what she loves. Likewise, she has neglected to love herself enough. Single women are not the only women that are not loving themselves enough. Just because you got the ring doesn't mean that you are loving yourself enough. The statement "happy wife happy life" means that a husband needs to do everything possible to make his woman happy so that they both can have a happy life. Of course, this is what we all want from our man. Still remember he is only human. He may have struggles of his own. He may not know how to do right by you because he's struggling trying to do right by himself. He may not know how to make you happy because he's struggling to make himself happy.

Please know that a man should not hold the keys to your mental stability. Do *you* want to be happy?! If so, why are you waiting for him to do it for you? Do you understand the burden it places on a man when he realizes that what he says or does determines your mood for the day? It's very unattractive, and it makes him walk on eggshells. For some men, the burden is too much to bear, and they choose to leave. I used to be that girl in marriage. Now, if my husband and I ever have a disagreement, I'll probably be upset for a little bit (the max probably an hour), and then I'm back to normal like nothing even happened.

Here's a hard truth a lot of women may find hard to accept. Man is not your life. Christ is your life (Colossians 3:4 KJV). Simply, because He said so. Also, because the minute a person becomes your life, they become your god. They control your every move, your every decision, your thoughts, and how you view yourself. If you feel they are your life, then without them, you feel you have no life. God forbid they were taken from the world, is that it for you in this world? I love my husband dearly; we are one. That's my partner in this life, and I wouldn't want it any other way. However, I can't allow him to be my god. Don't put that burden on your husband. Allow Him to reserve that space for God and watch how God teaches him how to be a better husband to you. Trust me, He can teach him better than you can.

Why aren't you pursuing your dreams, your passions, your goals, purpose? (Side note: Your husband will find you so much more attractive when he sees that you are passionate about something other than him.) It's a burning within you that wants you to go deeper and pursue greater. Is it lack of time? I've learned that you will never FIND time; you have to CREATE time.

With all that I mentioned above about the daily tasks of a wife, I went to the gym after I put my son down, entertained myself with my husband, and got to working on purpose. I was working in the wee hours of the night, although I still had to get up early. However, my vision was so REAL to me that I knew I had to create time. So, I worked on *me* at night, and I created time until purpose created time for me. Eventually, I left my nine to five job. You have to be intentional about the things you want in life. They won't just happen to you. Was I able to do this schedule every night? No! Sometimes, my body was too tired, and I had to listen to it. Yet, I would get back to doing it again.

Whatever you do, just don't stop; or you'll find yourself ten years later still at the same place. If the lack of money is the problem, push a little harder to bring in some extra cash. Your husband may be doing the best that he can. There are many ways to make money working on your own time that are super flexible. If you really want it, you'll do the research and find it. Seek and you shall find. Do what needs to be done so that you can be happy. Stop putting the burden on your husband. Because, ultimately, he'll do what he can, but until you're happy with yourself, you may never be satisfied with him.

Sometimes, women tend to blame their husbands because they've put all their energy into what their husband has going on. Then, if it gets nowhere, they blame him for their unhappiness. It's time to stop pointing the fingers. If two people are diligently working hard, strategizing, planning, and in peace together, something is bound to happen. Nonetheless, you must be honest with yourself. Are you guys working at it as a real business or as a hobby? Are you investing not only time but money? Could the problem be that you are trying to encourage your husband, but he doesn't appear to be encouraging himself? You're there to help with the purpose not the personality. You can't change a personality. If he doesn't have the drive, the motivation, the vision, or the will to work on purpose or a project, then you are investing your time into something that may not go anywhere. That is the time you get into prayer for your husband.

In the meantime, I would work on a project that is burning inside of you. I've seen that to motivate some men. In truth, people say that when you get married, you guys should have one purpose. It doesn't always work like that. Every relationship is different. A surgeon might not need his wife's help in the operating room. He may just need her help at home. While she is home, she can be building her project, passion, or purpose. A husband can be a pastor, and he may need her help there. If they work perfectly as a team, then that is perfect! If she believes she is called to be a speaker to women outside of the church as well, then go for it. With everything you're pursuing though, as a wife, make sure you take care of your family and home first. You WILL have time for you if you create it. How do I know? I used to be the woman that thought she didn't have time for herself. Thus, be the happy wife and enjoy your happy life. Just don't wait on anybody to do it for you.

NOTES TO
REMEMBER

——————

....

....

....

....

....

....

....

....

"Everything you want in life first begins with ME…
Yes, that means you."

CHAPTER 14

BE GOOD TO PEOPLE

The title of the book is *ME*. I'm basically referring to you. A lot of people may have picked up this book and believed it would be a book all about Judith - selfish almost. I used this title so that the woman reading this book can understand that she must be responsible for every decision that she makes in her life for her to be better and get better. Still, don't be deceived. To be the best "ME" you could be, you should do for people and be good to people. As I mentioned in prior chapters, you must love others as you love yourself. ME is just teaching you how to love yourself so that you can know how to love others with the same measure. You must be the best version of you so that you can give out the best version of you. It teaches you to be happy, to enjoy life, pursue greater, get better relationships, and not wait on people to do it for you.

In addition, if you have joy, peace, and a great life, you know how to give it to others. It could be monetary, advice, influence, or maybe even a hug. You should be so filled within yourself that you have more than enough to fill others. Do not be deceived to think that self-love is about being selfish. Because remember, your Father is in the people business. If He is no respecter of persons, why do you think He will not use you to bless others and others to bless you? He loves us all! In the process of you being good to people, don't ever forget about self-love. Don't love others more than you love yourself. Don't love others less than you love yourself. Love others as you love yourself. But please understand, you must first know how to love yourself enough, so that you can know how to love others in the same measure.

NOTES TO
REMEMBER

....

....

....

....

....

....

....

....

"Everything you want in life first begins with ME...
Yes, that means you."

CLOSING

I believe this book has helped you in many ways. If it did, be a blessing and share it with others because you want other women like you to be blessed as well. Follow me on my website, www.judithdials.com and subscribe to *Mature Enough* as I give relationship advice, inspirational messages, guides, videos, and e-books on how to be done with brokenness and obtain a life and relationship of pure inner happiness through email. Re-read this book for reminders of self-love. Continue your relationship with God by having constant communication. Continue finding out more about yourself and self-love.

I wrote this book because God has revealed to me the greatness of loving oneself enough, and I wanted to share it with the world. Still, I need to constantly be in communication with Him to learn more about self-love, my identity, how much He loves me, and who I am. I have not reached a level of "I've got it all" nor will anybody ever "have it all" unless they are God. I encourage you to continue to learn more about self-love, because as humans, we have weak moments and tend to forget who we are. Thus, we end up in bad situations. Conversely, constant communication with God allows Him to renew our mind every day, and it serves as a reminder. Yes, self-love is in everything. But, if you decide to stop your communication with God and seek more about self-love, then you missed it. Additionally, you'll once again find yourself in a broken life with broken relationships. You can't have self-love without God.

CONTACT
INFORMATION

Judith Dials
Author/Speaker/Relationship Coach

For Bookings, please contact Judith Dials at:
info@judithdials.com

Follow Judith Dials on Social Media:
Instagram: Judith Dials
Facebook: Judith Dials
Periscope: Judith Dials

www.judithdials.com

info@judithdials.com

"EVERYTHING
YOU WANT IN LIFE
FIRST BEGINS WITH
ME...
YES, THAT MEANS YOU!!!"

—JUDITH DIALS